DISABILITY:
FAITH AND ACCEPTANCE

PASTORAL CARE AND ETHICAL ISSUES

DISABILITY:
Faith and Acceptance

W Graham Monteith

THE SAINT ANDREW PRESS
· EDINBURGH ·

First published in 1987 by
THE SAINT ANDREW PRESS
121 George Street, Edinburgh EH2 4YN

Copyright © W Graham Monteith 1987

ISBN 0 7152 0614 1

Unless otherwise indicated, Scripture quotations are from the Good News
Bible (British usage edition), published by the Bible Societies and Collins,
© American Bible Society 1966, 1971, 1976. Used by permission.

The Statement on page 81 is from *Gathered for Life*, Official Report,
VI Assembly World Council of Churches, Vancouver, Canada 24 July – 10
August 1983. In fact, these were recommendations. Used by permission.

British Library Cataloguing in Publication Data
Monteith, W. Graham
    Disability : faith and acceptance. ——
    (Pastoral care and ethical issues).
    1. Handicapped —— religious life
    I. Title   II. Series
    248.8'6   BV4910

    ISBN 0–7152–0614–1

Contents

For my mother and late father

Author's Note

In 1979, I was asked by Dr Alan E Lewis to write an article on disability for the *New College Bulletin*. This book is simply an expansion of that article and therefore I must acknowledge the encouragement I received from him in showing an interest in the subject. As one of the few British academics writing in this field his influence can be found throughout my text.

Research has been difficult in such a remote area and I should like to mention three people who have helped me or guided me with research. They are Professor J K Mason, Professor D W D Shaw, and Jim Wallace MP.

I am indebted to two authors whose style and theories have influenced me. I acknowledge my dependence on Dorothee Sölle for a basic framework and to Harold H Wilke for demonstrating that a book on theology and disability can be written albeit from an American perspective. Finally, but certainly most importantly, I wish to thank Miss Marilyn Watters for her patient work in typing every word which has been dictated several times over. It has been a tremendous challenge to her and I have enjoyed working with her. My mother has also made it physically possible to write this book by acting as a 'human word-processor', correcting material, producing the index and advising on various paragraphs.

W Graham Monteith
Orkney, May 1987

7

Introduction

Few people with a disability can afford the luxury of writing a book. Life can be such a struggle that all energy is absorbed in day to day living. Even more energy is absorbed in coming to terms with the disability. I have been gifted with the promise of a life which is not a ceaseless struggle, and a mind which has been given time to indulge in thoughts about the meaning of life, its value and its worth. As the discussion unfolds in this book, I hope that it will be realised that I have found my answers in theology, and have decided to indulge myself and ask ultimate questions. In this book I will suggest certain reforms which are urgently required although I feel that someone with more strength and interest will have to carry them forward.

I am 40 years old, married, and have one son—Peter—who is not yet five years old. I was born in Glasgow to devoted parents who had the wide stable support of a large extended family. I lived a normal life, but that was only possible because of what my mother and father did for me. I could not toddle as a toddler, so my mother became my legs. I have never had the use of my right arm, so my father constructed my games for me. My speech was very difficult to understand, so my family gathered round to listen. My education had to be in Edinburgh at Westerlea School for Spastics, so my parents moved to Edinburgh.

At Westerlea, all the staff were pioneers. Cerebral Palsy may have been a very old condition, but the increased pressures from parents, the interest of charitable bodies, and of the medical profession, meant that great leaps were about to be taken in its treatment. I was one of only 20 lucky children who could be admitted to the school at that time, and over the next seven years of my life I would be taught to walk and to make some use of my hand. My speech was about to be reconstructed and my education begun in a classroom full of very primitive gadgets and a real loving care, where everything, right down to my desk, was made specially for me in order to control my involuntary movements which plague me to this day. The regime was not dissimilar to the much publicised treatment in Hungary, which to my great annoyance is being portrayed as new.

This was indeed a sheltered environment. Fortuitously my father was appointed headmaster of the Ross High School in Tranent. Tranent was at that time a mining village, riddled with disused mines and in consequence full of unstable foundations. For this reason the Ross High School never rose above two storeys and was ideal for someone who was mobile but with difficulty. Now I was a member of normal society, except that I was able to compensate for my disability by virtue of the fact that I was the headmaster's son. In a strange way I still miss the playground in which I never played, or the showers which were never needed because I never took part in games; but on the other hand I can give eternal thanks for the Domestic Science Cottage where I was able to dictate my exams in private. As I came to O Levels and Highers, I lulled the invigilator to sleep as I droned on to my mother.

I chose to study sociology and politics at Edinburgh University. I became deeply engrossed in my studies and engaged the help of many students who took notes for me. My mother, of course, continued to write my essays and my exams. It soon became known that I had good grades, and an almost photographic memory when it came to text books. I enjoyed considerable success academically.

However, all of this masked a deep sense of loss and of searching for identity. I very much wanted to attend all the parties the other students went to, and I had a great desire for a girlfriend. It is seldom possible for the non-handicapped to understand the pain and the agony of coming to terms with the opposite sex. The amount of energy which is taken up simply coming to terms with social limitations far out-strips the mental effort required to succeed academically.

I had many acquaintances but few friends. I had considerable success in student societies, but missed the warmth of everyday friendly activities.

I had a great capacity to appear happy, and to show a veneer of success. I believe that disabled people are very adept at this unfortunate technique. The modern jargon for it is 'over-compensating'. Appearing happy and successful, even foolhardy and courageous, creates the illusion of a 'tremendous spirit' within the disabled which I do not feel existed within myself, or within a great many of my disabled friends.

For my twenty-first birthday I was given the opportunity to go to America. My itinerary was carefully planned and enabled me to visit California and Canada. Perhaps I would have preferred a knapsack on my back and a Greyhound bus ticket in my hip pocket, but compromises always have to be made and they are invariably expensive. Flying was the only way such a trip was possible. Shortly after my return, I announced that I wished to study theology. Imagine the thought of all my education in sociology being in vain! However, sociology taught me how to be highly sceptical and I have remained so throughout my theological training and well into my ministry. At that time sociology was a most fashionable subject to study. Quite frankly, the Churches were besotted by the subject and I think this did me no harm. But, I cannot say that I find sociology a very satisfying subject in retrospect, and certainly do not find it of great use today.

After post-graduate study at the University of York I spent two years as an assistant minister in Drumchapel, a sprawling housing estate of 40 000 inhabitants in Glasgow, and from there I went to Berwick-upon-Tweed. This is not the appropriate place to discuss my ministry; that will appear in a different chapter. However, a few unrelated instances are worth a mention.

One year I crashed my invalid car in Edinburgh, and it was off the road for the best part of six months. Obviously this was not good enough and my parents decided to buy me a pavement buggy driven by battery. It was a great sign of growing maturity and acceptance actually to take this vehicle out on to the streets of Berwick wearing a dog collar and not to be embarrassed. In fact, one Sunday I went to church in my cassock in the buggy and was met by a student of photography who obviously thought this sight merited a photograph.

I have made regular visits to the General Assembly of the

Church of Scotland, and at each one I have spoken on some subject. But I always come away with a sickening feeling within me of failure. The Assembly Hall is not designed for the disabled, nor are my nerves designed to cope with addressing 1300 Commissioners. I have always felt that I have made an exhibition of myself, despite the fact that my comments attract coverage by some branches of the media. The Church of Scotland in common with most denominations has a long way to go before it can make the disabled feel free and accepted. In fairness those who know me make a tremendous effort to accommodate me, but I have been told by friends that this is not reflected in the rank and file of the General Assembly. So far the organisers have not been challenged to accommodate a wheelchair.

Finally, in this series of anecdotes, I would like to relate my feelings when the BBC's 'Songs of Praise' programme came from the Holy Trinity Church in Berwick. As one of the clergy I was placed with my wife in the choir stalls with a remote control camera very close to us. During the singing of 'The day thou gavest Lord has ended', this camera focussed on myself and my wife. I knew I had panicked, and as a result was sweating, grimacing and showing considerable involuntary movements. So be it. But I would ask the reader to imagine how I felt when the verse concerned was re-shot. Such occurrences make me envious of those who can appear publicly without fear of the occasion betraying their tension as it did mine. I feel that as the public and the media understand more about disability they will not find it necessary to hide such distressing features.

I married Angela in 1981; and on 1 August 1982, Peter was baptised. Both services took place in Wallace Green Church, Berwick-upon-Tweed. Marriage ought to signal an intimacy which should be the greatest form of acceptance. In this, and especially in the acceptance of a child in innocence and naïveté, I have found my greatest reward. Remember that many disabled people wait a long time to receive such intimacy from someone other than close family. The opportunity to build one's own family is a gift which is received with the greatest humility and sense of privilege.

There are many books written on the theme of the disabled

and marriage and sex. I do not intend to comment on them in this book. I must however confess that when a disabled person does marry, he shares his disability with his spouse. He or she takes upon his or herself the burden of the handicap. There is a sense in which marriage with all its joys is made difficult by the demands of disability. Getting to know the limitations of your partner is a challenge to the non-handicapped partner. In the first months of marriage, I was more aware of my disability than I had ever been before. Through time this gradually abated. But it continued to arise in my consciousness now and again.

Such an obvious occasion is when one contemplates bringing up a child. I was not going to be able to lift the baby out of his cot, change nappies, or bath him; and I was going to have to fight for the first opportunity to look after Peter myself. With the great freedom of Orkney, I can now look after him all day myself, and can indeed fly to Edinburgh with him by myself. These freedoms would probably not have existed outside this tranquil island.

Peter was born on 24 June 1982. It was the day that the news of the disaster at Bluff Cove in the Falklands was first broadcast on our television. I cried a lot that day; I cried because of the stark contrast between the loss of life, the disfigurement of those soldiers, and the life that I had just seen born. I cried also because I had always had an ambition to present my mother and father with a grandchild who was not disabled. I remember having this feeling from teenage days, and now I was able to rejoice in the gift.

Five days later, I wept in anguish. My father died in Berwick Infirmary after a massive heart attack. It seemed to me that the gift that had been offered to all of us had now been denied to him; it seemed also that I had demanded too much of him, in care and support in the last few weeks.

Have I ever had a spiritual crisis? Have I ever blamed God for my disability? Have I ever asked whether God is totally unjust? Have I ever thought that Christian virtues are not the best way to survive in this brutal world? My answer must be that the only time this has occurred was at the end of that week of intense joy and sorrow. I was saved from the abyss by the thought that our relationship with God is not static, but is always changing. God relates to us in a different way every day, but never deserts us. God is constant; it is me who has to change. I received many letters of condolence; one in particular from a fellow minister helped me more than any. It ended with the last sentence of Matthew's Gospel, as translated by William Barclay: 'And there is not a day when I will not be with you to the end of time'. On the day of my father's death, the Presbytery of Duns nominated me as its Moderator for the year 1982/83.

This very personal introduction is coming to a close. I wish to relate a few more anecdotes. There is much I could say about marriage, but I think it is important simply to pick instances which have influenced the thinking of this book.

Angela and I have discussed disability at great length. Sometimes people have tense arguments which have eventually bubbled over into print. Whilst Angela was expecting Peter, there was much correspondence, in the local paper in Berwick, about the issues of life and death, and of abortion. Both of us rapidly became exasperated by propaganda being put out through this paper by the Society for the Protection of the Unborn Child (SPUC), the local priest — for whom we had a high regard — and from the Convent nearby. We wrote a letter to the press stating that if we knew that the baby which Angela was carrying was to be born deformed or disabled, we would seriously consider terminating the pregnancy. The letter further went on to argue that my life may not have been considered worth saving, if it had been possible to detect disability within me before birth 40 years ago. The letter, I think, embarrassed many people, hurt my mother and father, and only elicited one note of congratulations from a doctor involved with family planning. I do not think that I would adhere to that letter now. Every time I look at Peter I am forced to an opposite conclusion, although I still do not accept the arguments of the pro-life lobby.

A year later the Church of Scotland was deeply divided. The question which divided it was whether two convicted criminals should be admitted to the ministry. I consistently supported these men and would do so to this day. Angela, on the other hand, did not consider that they should have been admitted to the ministry and still holds that view. The basis of my argument was that these men carried with them a stigma and that this stigma could be as debilitating as that of the stigma of disability. The Church seemed equally reluctant to accept either, whilst it bears a responsibility to accept both. My particular defence of these men caused much reaction within my own circles and in *Life and Work*, the record of the Church of Scotland. I had to explain that very often the disabled were like groups in society fighting for acceptance. Often I have had to compare myself to a black in America, or a woman suffering discrimination. Now I dared to suggest that I suffered the same discrimination as a criminal.

Another fault was that I used the word 'stigma'. This word will occur again in this book and I want to make it clear that it implies no disgrace to carry a stigma; it is simply a mark. A mark can be sometimes ugly; but it can also be sometimes beautiful, as were the marks which Jesus showed to Thomas.

One time my wife and I wrote a letter which was never printed. We wrote from the island of Mull to the Editor of the Church magazine in Berwick. We were tired and perhaps forgot the kindness of the office-bearers whose congregation we were about to address. In that letter we complained of many things. But most of all we complained of the seeming lack of compassion within the congregation. Their inability to babysit, to ask us out and to visit us in the manse, were our main complaints. The letter was really quite bitter. In a sentence, we were saying that the congregation owed us a living. We had not learned the secret of give and take; of the kind of barter we were later to experience in Orkney, for example. Subsequently I have also discovered that this is a common feeling in the ministry and often leads to 'ministerial burnout'.

The day after we wrote that letter, we went to a small hamlet called Kintra on the Ross of Mull. After spending half an hour there we got into the car to leave and I found that Angela was in tears. She had fallen in love with the beauty and peace of the island, and with this spot in particular. From that time forward I sought to find an island charge; and so I write this book from the island of Hoy which is the southern-most and largest island in Orkney. I find now that I am becoming intolerant of those who live at the pace of the cities, or those who are condescending to my disability, or those who do not realise that I am living the same life that they live, and that I face the same elements which they face. Our journey to the islands was a good one. I have never found such acceptance anywhere and I bless the day that we went to Kintra.

The reader might well be forgiven for considering that he has just read a school essay masquerading as an autobiography. This is not the point of the introduction. I would compare the introduction to an overture. Within the theme are woven the main arias and choruses which are going to occur within the plot. My account has been very selective. Contained within these stories are the themes and preoccupations of this book.

I have tried in vain to draft this book objectively without reference to my own experience. This proved to be a fruitless task and has been abandoned. I must explain that the book deals with aspects of disability of which I am aware. I am not acquainted, nor do I have any real experience of mental handicap, and I find that my heart rests mainly with people who have congenital conditions other than mental, such as my own. I must apologise for my blind spots and trust that I can share a few worthwhile insights.

Part One

1

Disabled People Bound by Society; Freed by Christ

The disabled are people. The International Year of the Disabled Person was held in 1981. Many books were written at the time, and the public were made aware of the needs of people with disabilities. It was unfortunate that the year was referred to very often as 'The International Year of the Disabled'. Well-wishers and organisations learned a lot about physical and mental disability, they contributed a lot of money to it, they even adapted buildings to accommodate the disabled; but very often they forgot the actual people behind their objectives. The people concerned were lively, vibrant personalities. They shared—in common with the rest of mankind—the frustrations of life, its disappointments, and its many joys. Emotionally, and in many cases physically, they could not escape pain and suffering. Their loved ones watched with an intensity of anxiety which few other groups in society experience. In this group of people throughout the world, there were children who had been born with a disability; there were adults who had been snatched from a very active life into the clutches of a wheelchair by an accident; there were also other adults who had been smitten with a progressive disease they had not known earlier in life—such as multiple sclerosis; there were old people who were suffering from arthritis, the crippling effects of a stroke, or the closing-in of their world as they lost sight or hearing: they were 'the disabled'. They needed help, but each one of them also wanted to be recognised and valued as an individual. Their disability could inflict upon them great financial hardship, isolation from their friends, or a deep insecurity within their lives. However well they seemed to accept these signs of suffering or affliction, often this could only be mitigated by the comfort of acceptance by their friends.

Why does God allow this? Does he create it? Does he inflict suffering? These are not the questions which are normally asked in books about disability. The fact that they are asked implies a two-pronged attack. We must *first* ask ourselves what it means to be disabled—a task which can be undertaken from any point of view. *Second*, we must recognise that we are dealing with human souls who can respond in grace to God's love or reject God because of the resentments engendered by the affliction he may seem to have imposed. This is precisely the subject of the story of Job, and his situation is not dissimilar to that of many disabled people. Christians must be aware of the nature of disability whilst also being aware of God's providence. Our understanding of disability has to be deepened by our faith in God's providence. Therefore it is important that we must address ourselves to a brief definition of disability, and then understand what it means to be disabled in a world ruled by God. Secular language and sacred language will come together in Job's anguish.

Since 1971 three words—'impairment', 'disability' and 'handicap'—have been essential to any understanding of people who have disabilities. These words are quoted in any later definition of disability.[1] Most people understand what it means to suffer an 'impairment'. This term covers any defect relevant to our normal functioning. It can involve as little as a set of false teeth, or the full malfunctioning of the nervous system as in the case of cerebral palsy. Society's experience of impairment is so widespread that the term is open to much abuse. It is widely misused by the sympathetic well-wisher and by fairly militant disabled people alike.[2] 'We are all disabled in some way', is a very common statement and a well meant form of comfort. Such thinking is far from a full understanding of disability. Can it be said with any honesty that someone suffering from a peptic ulcer is disabled or handicapped when it can be rectified with drugs and a little care?

Let us now imagine someone who has a severely broken leg. The doctors say that with time the leg will heal and there will be very little evidence of the injury. This man happens to live in a bungalow next door to the shop which he owns. The pub is not too far away, nor is the church which he never attends anyway. For the time of his convalescence he can hobble to work, find his way around the village, and meet his friends in the pub who think his ski-ing accident is a great joke in any case. It would appear that our friend is very far from disabled. Inconvenienced yes, but not greatly affected in his lifestyle, although he has had to give up 'keep fit' classes for the time being. The fact to be noted is that this rather severe impairment has not disabled this man at all because his life has not been significantly altered.

It is not, however, such a happy tale for those whom we normally think of as being disabled.

A real disability deprives a sufferer of some functional ability. Perhaps one is confined to a wheelchair; another lacks muscular co-ordination; and yet another becomes dependent on a guide dog. The loss of function can vary greatly, from those already mentioned to less apparent ones such as incontinence or the classic example of deafness. Your wheelchair, or spastic movements and difficulty in walking, affects the way you live, your capacity to work, and to meet with friends. The man with the broken leg may well have been unable to go to work if he had to commute to the nearest city; he may have found himself unable to live at home successfully had he lived in a flat; and his friends might not have seen the inconvenience caused as a joke but more as a reason for shunning him.

Typically, the disabled person finds it hard to seek employment and to overcome the prejudice of employers. His wheelchair creates an immediate barrier to many public buildings and his need for adaptations makes life very costly. Most disabilities can be overcome, but at quite a cost financially. The government only really recognises the following as worthy of grants: severe lack of mobility; the need for constant attendance because of the possibility of self-inflicted danger; or constant help with toiletting needs. But clothes, special furniture, adaptations to houses, and many more things, also make life extremely costly. Income for the disabled is a constant source of worry. Understandably, most attention is paid to those on the poverty line—on sickness benefit or supplementary benefit with additional allowances; nevertheless it would appear that a much more radical approach is needed to embrace disabled people who are not poor, yet who cannot enjoy the fruits of their earnings because they are spent on very functional and necessary luxuries. What may be a luxury to someone without a disability becomes a necessity. You cannot choose whether to use the call-box 50 yards from home instead of owning a telephone.

About 20 years ago it was more fashionable to talk of the 'handicapped' rather than the 'disabled'. Now it is widely recognised that many people can be disabled without being greatly handicapped and vice-versa. The word 'handicapped' has taken on a specific meaning since the seventies. It refers to that part of life which is lost because of societal functions. The most important area of concern for the disabled has been access. Much of the effort of those concerned with disability has been to produce accessible buildings, accessible not only for someone in a wheelchair to enter, but also so that once inside a building one can use all the facilities. This means that a building must have lower counters, adequate toilet facilities, lifts, and many other amenities the lack of which would deprive the disabled person of the enjoyment of that building for entertainment, work or pleasure. It has already been said by Peter Large that we live in a 'neurotic' society, that our concern for fire regulations and many other such measures of safety exclude the disabled from theatres, cinemas, and many other public buildings.[3] Disabled people are also deprived of transport, they are often given inadequate opportunity to train for work and to achieve a post; and they are very often left without the possibility of developing social skills because their limitations become burdens to their friends and acquaintances. Every time society prevents a disabled person from doing something, either because of physical or psychological barriers, *society* is handicapping that person considerably.

Disability and Suffering

The Book of Job is a poem about a man who has to come to terms with disability, his own righteousness and the supposed neglect of God. The book was written at a time when the prophets were mainly concerned with the righteousness of nations and with God's justice in dealing with them. It addressed itself more to the dealings of God with the individual rather than to national concerns and state religion. Job finds it very difficult to accept that he has been disabled by God and now he questions God's justice and the value of life itself.[4]

We must now wrestle with God and trust that we can find a solution to this vexing question of how God can love us yet allow so much suffering through disability. Job's sentiments are echoed in the folklore and poetry of much of Middle Eastern culture at the time when the book was written. Simone Weil terms incessant suffering as 'affliction'. The pain one suffers with toothache is not in the same category because it can be relieved very quickly in much the same way as the symptoms of any other temporary impairment. According to Weil, there are three components of an affliction: they are the physical, the psychological and the social.[5] These components are all present in the life of someone who is both disabled and handicapped. There is a great deal of physical pain; while we can quantify the pain of arthritis or of common back conditions, we should never forget the pains which come from lack of co-ordination. Bumping into things can be very painful, and these pains are often understated by those who suffer. The psychological tension must already be apparent. These particular pains arise with the deprivation caused when one cannot function in a certain way which society demands. Social pains are those where people are so handicapped by the restraints put upon them by society that they feel left out or forgotten. The word 'affliction' therefore covers the depth of suffering experienced in disability. It suggests to us that the disabled could well be tormented as Job was, physically, psychologically and socially.

In the Book of Job, chapter 2, we learn how he suffers physical pain in attempting in vain to cure the sores which had appeared all over his body. We find repeated evidence that he was suicidal and how he was advised by his comforter not to worry himself to death with resentment. Resentment is a very powerful and often destructive sentiment in the psyche of disabled people. Finally, Job is struck by the loss of confidence which he has in his friends, his prosperity, and closeness to those whom he had previously trusted. The pain, anxiety and the anger which his affliction engenders makes

Job ask ultimate questions—questions which we must ask as we stand with the disabled person who is discontented and restless in the pain of his affliction.

Job's sentiments are reflected in modern society. More and more people drift from institutional religion as they see the suffering of the world unfold before them on the television screen. How can God allow my loved one to die in such pain? Does he exist as a God of love? We read increasingly of organisations such as Exit (the voluntary euthanasia society) which claim to have members who believe that an end to their sufferings should be available through voluntary euthanasia. Like Job they are assumed to long for the day of their death.

Disabled people cannot dare to have faith without asking these ultimate questions and finding solutions which reinforce their faith. One commentator contends that 'Job is another Jacob who, in wrestling with the deity, says in effect, "I will not let thee go except thou bless me"'.[6] Every Christian who genuinely seeks to live with disability must be prepared to wrestle with God and to be driven by a spirit of enquiry. The true and sympathetic reader must learn of God's desertion before seeking the comfort of the risen Christ.

The first and most important contention of this book is that disabled people live a life as part of society. The degree of their disability, of their suffering, is dependent upon how they are accepted and offered a place in the lives of others. The unease felt by society is directly correlated to the understanding of the tension which exists within the disabled person and his loved ones.

Job cried from the depth of his despair:

> Human life is like forced army service,
>   like a life of hard manual labour,
>   like a slave longing for cool shade;
>   like a worker waiting for his pay.
> Month after month I have nothing to live for;
>   night after night brings me grief.

(Job 7:1–3)

The reader must accept the challenge of understanding the *ennui*, the *angst*, the despair or the anxiety of the afflicted before he can continue on a pilgrimage to find constructive reasons for living within the Christian faith.

The Bible and Disability

We have seen that disability can be defined both medically and poetically in the case of Job. Let us now examine some difficult passages from scripture. The Bible offers much evidence that the people of God could not come to terms with disability; and it also offers much in the way of opportunity for any person to vent his anger at God, blaming him for the lifestyle to which they have been condemned.

American people and American Churches have been much more aware of disabled people and much more willing to speak of the prejudice Christians and Jews have shown towards disability. There are, of course, very real and valid objections to some of the statutes recorded in the *Torah*, but there is also a sense in which the language is offensive in the same way as sexist language is offensive to some women. The most famous statute from Leviticus referring to disability reads as follows:

> 'None of your descendants who has any physical defect ['blemish', RSV] may present the food-offering to me. This applies for all time to come. No man with any physical defect may make the offering: no one who is blind, lame, disfigured, or deformed; no one with a crippled hand or foot; no one who is a hunchback or a dwarf; no one with any eye or skin disease: and no eunuch. No descendant of Aaron the priest who has any physical defect may present the food-offering to me. Such a man may eat the food offered to me, both the holy food-offering and the very holy food-offering, but because he has a physical defect, he shall not come near the sacred curtain or approach the altar. He must not profane these holy things, because I am the Lord and I make them holy.'
>
> (Lev. 21:17–23)

One can well imagine that in an agrarian society many of the disfigurements mentioned in this passage must have posed considerable threats. None but the perfect could act as priests. There were many elaborate acts and rituals to perform in the event of some unclean act occurring, and only the cleanest were considered fit to minister.

We can call the marks described in this passage, 'blemishes', 'stigmas' or 'black spots'. It seems quite clear that the language of the Old Testament speaks in such a way that the disabled are excluded from the cult and from many rôles in society.

Disabled churchmen and women in America have tried very successfully to overcome these barriers, some of which still exist into the twentieth century, lingering (in the same way as anti-Semitism) in the sub-conscious of the Church. They are slowly winning the battle in Church and liberal Synagogue alike.

Harold H Wilke, an American theologian who has been disabled since birth, argues that findings from the *Talmud* appear to support a more compassionate case for the disabled. The findings suggest that if the stigma a potential priest carried was not likely to cause offence, then the ban could be lifted and he could enter the office and serve the congregation.[7]

This line of argument carried two very interesting questions to those who are asked to accept disabled people in positions of authority in the Church today, and these questions can be expanded to almost any office. *First*, it is widely recognised that one of the most important truths to understand about disabled people is that there is no uniform disability. That their disability is a blemish or a stigma is beyond doubt. However, it is sometimes totally invisible: in the case of someone who has a record of psychiatric illness for instance; or in the case of those whom society would wish to dismiss as being beyond the pale, or beyond normal accepted behaviour. If there is such diversity it means that our sensitivity has to be raised to such an awareness that we can accept such people because of their potential, whilst at the same time not being prejudiced by a particular disability or indeed by our secret knowledge of such a disability.

People suffering from cerebral palsy have great variations in their disabilities, both mental and physical. Some have physical capabilities and a range of mobility quite impossible to others. I am often amused by the number of people who think they have seen me when they are actually thinking of other spastics in public life. Sometimes I know immediately the person they are thinking of and am aware that they see our disabilities as the same although our physical difficulties are quite different. Fortunately, I was able to have a car adapted; and only those who understand cerebral palsy would appreciate the benefit I derived from this.

The tragedy behind the 'does he take sugar' syndrome is that the majority of people are not willing to venture behind the façade, the visible stigma, to discover what lies behind it, and how fruitful and gifted the personality of that person may be.

Several polls have shown that when people are asked the question 'Who are the disabled?', generally around 70 per cent think of people in wheelchairs. Next on the list come the blind and the handicapped at about 27 per cent. If people are left to describe the disabled in their own way, 17 per cent describe them as 'People who can't look after themselves'.[8] The public do not share the definition of this book; they see disability as paralysis, amputation, and the type of condition that comes later in life. They use the word 'handicapped' to describe congenital defects. On the whole their perception is very generalised and undiscriminating.

We live in a society which is just as impatient with the imperfect as in biblical times. Every advertisement which encroaches into our personal life at home portrays a perfection which is sadly lacking in disabled people and even in normal people. There is after all no perfect female figure, an image of manliness which is universal, nor a perfect way to bring up a child portrayed with parents without financial worries, and domestic chores which impose no strain whatsoever. Disabled people simply do not have a rôle in such a society, and in its own insidious way the media imposes Levitical law upon all that carry a stigma.

Second, how far are Christians willing to go to look behind a person's stigma, blemish or disability? Disabled people are taught from a very early age that they must meet people 'more than half way'. Whilst such advice is both commendable and practical, it would be good if we could reverse it. If Christians could find it within their powers to accept the disabled by putting in much of the effort themselves it would considerably ease the disabled person's burden. We must learn to accept in our fellowship those who look vastly dif-

ferent from ourselves, perhaps have less developed personalities, shyness, or even an overbearing ability to compensate
for their disability by dominating the company. Often in the
search for acceptance the disabled person does not credit the
able-bodied with the ability to see their needs. They themselves are only too willing to divide the world into two parts—
the disabled world and the non-disabled world. Many fellowships are also so close knit that it is possible for the disabled
person to be impeded in many different ways from entering
into that fellowship because it involves too many disruptions
to what are already the dynamics of the situation.

One story in the Acts of the Apostles illustrates how the
love of Jesus Christ has greatly mitigated the strictures of
Levitical law. We read in Acts 8, vv 28–38 about the encounter Philip had with the Ethiopian eunuch. This man was
deeply absorbed with the scriptures of the Old Testament, in
particular the Servant Songs of Isaiah. The scriptures, however, exclude him from the Old Israel. He asked Philip, 'What
is to keep me from being baptized?' And the love of God in
Christ now surrounded this man who previously had been
barred from entering fully into both his understanding of
scriptures and his fellowship with the body of early Christians.

A woman stood hesitantly in front of a church notice board
in Glasgow, asking herself, 'How can I have my child baptised?' She was staring at the notice board *pretending* to read it
because in actual fact she was illiterate. But the church took
her in, made her welcome, and set the seal of God's love on
her baby.

The case of the healing of the man born blind is one of the
most vexing passages in the New Testament. It is not acceptable to the modern mind that sin causes illness, nor is it
healthy to think of the sins of parents being visited upon their
children. But even our modern knowledge of the effects of
smoking, drugs and alcohol on the health of a pregnant
woman and of her fetus is not really a new insight into the
guilty feelings which lie behind this story. The most we can
say is that all parents should be responsible for seeking the
best perinatal care available, and for taking every precaution
that is advised or which they see fit. Several years ago, the
Spastics Society ran a campaign entitled 'Save a Baby'. This

campaign involved a petition to the government seeking more adequate perinatal care and pointing towards France as an example of a country where perinatal care is given a very much higher priority in all classes of society. In other words, our modern minds are not concerned with sin but with a concern for care, involvement and a knowledge of the development of a pregnancy.

We must approach the passage in St John's Gospel with an open mind, attempting to understand what is behind the thinking of the Scribes, the Pharisees and Jesus, and come to an enlightened understanding of the purpose of our Lord. The passage reads:

> As Jesus was walking along, he saw a man who had been born blind. His disciples asked him, 'Teacher, whose sin caused him to be born blind? Was it his own or his parents' sin?'
>
> Jesus answered, 'His blindness has nothing to do with his sins or his parents' sins. He is blind so that God's power might be seen at work in him. As long as it is day, we must keep on doing the work of him who sent me; night is coming when no one can work. While I am in the world, I am the light for the world.'
>
> After he said this, Jesus spat on the ground and made some mud with the spittle; he rubbed the mud on the man's eyes and said, 'Go and wash your face in the Pool of Siloam'. (This name means 'Sent'.) So the man went, washed his face, and came back seeing.
>
> His neighbours, then, and the people who had seen him begging before this, asked, 'Isn't this the man who used to sit and beg?'
>
> (John 9:1–8)

The way Jesus handles this question can be a great source of comfort to parents who are confused and bewildered by the birth of a malformed child. Jesus states quite categorically that sin does not come into reckoning. The parents of this child, or any other child, have no cause to feel guilt or remorse; and yet at the same time they should recognise God's hand in control of the situation. In this passage, it is suggested that God has caused this blindness for his own purpose. This is an incorrect interpretation. The passage concludes that God's glory can be shown in this situation; but this is not a reference to a pre-ordained disability nor to suffering which is put before Jesus as material for a miracle, but to God's control of the situation as revealed in his Son's compassion and ability to pronounce forgiveness of sins. That is to say, Christ brings wholeness into the situation where others have failed. Christ was the last resort for these parents, and in Christ they found that God was in control, and, through the love of Jesus, God nurtured and developed a mature attitude in their minds and in the mind of society which offered them an ability to live both with this child and with his disability.

God's mission and purpose for all mankind, no matter what their condition, was so told in Isaiah and adopted and made effective by Christ's declaration of his own ministry in Luke:

> Then Jesus went to Nazareth, where he had been brought up, and on the Sabbath he went as usual to the synagogue. He stood up to read the Scriptures and was handed the book of the prophet Isaiah. He unrolled the scroll and found the place where it is written,
> 'The Spirit of the Lord is upon me,
>> because he has chosen me to bring good news to the poor.
> He has sent me to proclaim liberty to the captives and re-covery of sight to the blind;
> to set free the oppressed
>> and announce that the time has come when the Lord will save his people.'
>
> (Luke 4:16–19)

There is a relationship in the passages we have examined between a person's impairment and disability and, more importantly, his handicap. Within the miracles of Jesus, we find fairly consistent reference to impairment. Jesus heals blindness, leprosy, lameness and various psychological disturbances. His contemporaries were probably aware that people suffering from these conditions were disabled in that they were deprived of many functions. The disabled in biblical times, as in many parts of the Third World today, did not have access to welfare facilities such as those of this country and other Western countries. Their plight was such that it was not particularly important that people thought of how society was handicapping them.

However, it appears that Jesus repeatedly released people from the laws that bound them to their condition, and in so doing he freed them from their handicap. The Ethiopian eunuch was handicapped because his society forbade his access to high Jewish office; the early Church released him. And the blind man was no longer an object of scorn or ambiguous belief, but was freed to live within his society. Jesus' ministry espoused freedom for all to live and work under God's rule. Not only were people's impairments miraculously removed, but with the miracle came a new social structure. Their disabilities were within the power of God, and God's power through Jesus was entirely directed at releasing people for a new and active life in Christ.

Notes to Chapter 1

1 A I Harris (*et al*) *Handicapped and Impaired in Great Britain* (Part 1) (HMSO, London, 1971)
2 Allan T Sutherland, *Disabled We Stand* (Human Horizon Series) (Souvenir Press Ltd, London, 1981), p 20
3 Silver Jubilee Committee on Improving Access for Disabled People, *Can Disabled People Go Where You Go?* (DHSS, London, 1979)
4 William B Stevenson, *The Poem of Job* (The British Academy, London, 1947)
5 Simone Weil, *The Love of God and Affliction: Waiting for God* (G P Putman and Sons, New York, 1951), p 117
6 Emil G Kraeling, *The Book of the Ways of God* (SPCK, London, 1938), p 231
7 Harold H Wilke, *Creating the Caring Congregation* (Abingdon Press, Nashville, 1980), p 23 ff
8 Roy McConkey and Bob McCormack, *Breaking Barriers* (Souvenir Press Ltd, London, 1983), p 36 ff

2

Abortion: The Compassionate Exception

The doctrine of creation is central to our faith. We proclaim that God creates everything, and that there is nothing in this world that is not within his power. It is all too simple to regard creation as being summed up in Genesis, without considering carefully the process of creation. God creates even today, and is creating at all times. The Scriptures offer us the vision of the beginning, the process and the end. A God whose world has fallen must first redeem it, and in so doing he has brought to the minds of the Prophets a world with a different order of nature, and through Christ to the early Christians a vision of the new Jerusalem more majestic than Solomon's Temple. Amidst the complexities of today's life, we must never forget that we live under God's providence, and that as new opportunities unfold for us we must ourselves see how God is expecting us to act in his creation which is always changing.

Psalm 139 is often used as a text for proof of God's care from conception to the grave. The part which interests us begins at verse 13:

> You created every part of me;
>> you put me together in my mother's
>> womb.
> I praise you because you are to be
>> feared;
>> all you do is strange and wonderful.
>> I know it with all my heart.
> When my bones were being formed,
>> carefully put together in my mother's
>> womb,
> when I was growing there in secret,
>> you knew that I was there —
>> you saw me before I was born.

The days allotted to me
  had all been recorded in your book,
  before any of them ever began.

(Ps. 139:13–16)

The entire psalm is a testimony to God's omnipotence, omnipresence and omnificence.[1] There is no place in which man can escape God's knowledge: his power surrounds man's path through life; even in the secrecy of the womb he is creative. This is a vital passage to anyone who considers life from conception to be sacred. And there are other passages which in some way or another refer back to the womb: for example there is the promise of Jeremiah that he was singled out from the beginning of his life for his prophetic rôle (see Jer. 1:5). Presumably at each point in Jeremiah's life, God thus provided the means to his eventual call as a prophet. It can be argued that his eventual rôle was not pre-ordained, but that the statement testifying to this was based on a retrospective examination of his life and circumstances up until that time. Disabled people can also look retrospectively and rationalise and identify the providential rôle which God has played in placing them in society.

Of course, in the Book of Job we can find negative references to the prenatal state (Job 3:11):

I wish I had died in my mother's womb
  or died the moment I was born.

or again (Job 10:18–19):

Why, God, did you let me be born?
  I should have died before anyone saw me.
To go from the womb straight to the grave
  would have been as good as never existing.

These verses from Job illustrate how it is possible to look retrospectively at one's life and question one's very existence. They suggest that whenever we wish to account for God's providence we can only do so with the wisdom of years of hindsight.

To regard life as an act of creation without a process is to deny the providence of God, happiness, and the developing of a quality of life out of a difficult situation. A rigid view of creation limits the potentiality of inner development in one's life, thereby placing all the onus of perception on the spectator. This will be a major argument in the next chapter. However, complete faith in God's providence is to accept that we live in order to make decisions, radically to mould and shape our existence, prayerfully and intently within the will of God. Man came of age not with Bonhoeffer but with Kierkegaard, who demonstrated that faith and obedience lead to tensions which make life adventurous. He demonstrated that the modern man lives in the present and is moulded by God as long as he continues to respond. It was only in retrospect that Isaac could see how God provided for his father's needs in obedience to God's command to offer him as a sacrifice, and he was spared at the last moment by the provision of a ram. Isaac's historical rôle in the Bible can be seen to emanate from the care God showed precisely at the time of extreme danger.

Psalm 139 testifies to the confidence its writer has in God. The psalmist never has been deserted, he always has had the benefit of God's guidance, and he was aware that at no stage had he been outside God's power. Such an experience is common to many, including many disabled people. However, the psalm was written after the writer had realised the truth of God's presence. Nowadays the psalms can be used readily in devotional literature and in scriptural counselling. There are many texts which speak about God's constancy and God's love, and these are very easily quoted in times of need, common distress, or buoyant jubilation. They do not in themselves represent a corpus of theology, but a testament to the writer's experiences of God.

The Bible undoubtedly is a great source of comfort and of guidance to many. The Church, however, in a period of retrenchment against the secularism of the past few decades is tempted to become authoritarian, and to use biblicism as a warrant for such an approach. The way of the Cross may remain central to conservative evangelicals, but this does not seem to be alive with the pathos and agony which that way entailed to Jesus and to all who follow it. The Church tends rather to attempt to find authority in certain areas of life where it claims to have an exclusive comment to make. Pro-life organisations in this country and the 'moral majority' in the USA are setting up a strong and well orchestrated campaign against permissive legislation governing abortion. Much of their campaign is justifiable in the light of over-permissiveness and our society's interpretation of the law. However, the concern of pro-life campaigns with the disabled by-passes complex scientific matters and medical ethics. Potential parents of congenitally disabled children may be affected greatly by this campaign and we must seek therefore to offer them a mature approach to this difficult area of their lives.

Parents of a child who is congenitally deformed suddenly find that their lives are changed. Perhaps at no other time in a marriage is optimism so high as in the anticipation of a coming birth; yet in the background there may also be anxiety, and for many reasons the mother's emotions are heightened. When, in these circumstances, the parents have to come to terms with the fact that the child is deformed, the effect can be quite horrendous. It can lead to feelings of remorse, of guilt, even to rejection of the child and often to post-natal depression in the mother. The complications of plans for the care of a normal child have gone ahead, and now many other plans have to be made very quickly. There may be a long stay in hospital. There may be the need to alter the nursery to accommodate the demands, and relatives and friends have to be told. The other mothers in the ward will return to their clinics and peer groups, with experiences to relate and knowledge to be gained. The mother of a disabled child searches for a charity who will help her to understand her child's condition, its likely development, and to give her support in her isolation.

There are several ways in which congenital deformity can come about. *First*, there is deformity caused by damage before, during, or after birth; cerebral palsy or certain other forms of brain damage come into this category. *Second*, there are diseases which are known to be attributable to genetic disorders. These include Down's syndrome, haemophilia and muscular dystrophy. *Third*, there are diseases which are still being researched and which require considerable sums of money to be spent to find a cause, for instance, of cystic fibrosis or spina bifida. Disabilities caused by damage may be eradicated or reduced by better perinatal care. Those which are genetically caused are those most affected by the issues surrounding abortion and genetic counselling.

Of all the illnesses caused by genetic disorders, those most affected by attitudes towards abortion are those which can be detected by tests. These mainly centre on Down's syndrome and spina bifida. Medical science has now given us the ability to detect many of these conditions in the fetus, and will go on providing more reliable indicators to parents. The result is that the opposition to abortion which used to be concerned mainly about 'abortion on demand' is now deeply concerned about these tests and their ethical implications.

The Abortion Act of 1967 was introduced by a son of the manse. The Act did not legalise abortion, but stated the conditions under which a termination could be made.[2] According to the Act, two physicians must agree and certify that termination is necessary, because in their opinion, formed in good faith, the following applies:

> (a) The continuance of the pregnancy would involve risk to the life of the pregnant woman, or injury to the physical or mental health of the pregnant woman or any existing children of her family, greater than if the pregnancy were terminated; or
> (b) That there is a substantial risk that if the child were born it would suffer from such physical or mental abnormalities as to be seriously handicapped.

Clause (a) has been greatly abused over the years. For a time, Britain was a haven for women seeking an abortion. It has been impossible to define 'physical or mental health'. The majority of abortions are carried out under this clause. Judges have pointed out that a great deal of investigation ought to go into a mother's health in order to justify an abortion on these grounds.[3] When the Act came into being, tests to detect a physical abnormality were not so readily available, but the case of the potential hazard to an embryo consequent to a mother contracting rubella might be an example of what was in mind.

The availability of screening for spina bifida and Down's syndrome has now altered the situation dramatically. Most mothers who may be at risk because of their age, or even because of regional variations in probability, are offered the amniocentesis test, and are usually expected to accept an abortion if the test is positive. The test draws off small quantities of amniotic fluid from the womb which will contain telltale signs of deformity, such as cells which escape from the open lesion in the spine of a fetus with spina bifida. The ability to forecast to parents the likelihood of spina bifida, or Down's syndrome, has radically altered the psychology behind the two clauses. It is now possible to argue that society has taken upon itself the right to eliminate disability by what some would call 'eugenic' abortion.

Such an argument has disturbed many physicians and parents alike. Professor R B Zachery describes the quality of life which can be offered to a child suffering from spina bifida; and he then disallows the right to deny life to one such. He argues:

> The attitude of mind that would eliminate all the severely handicapped reminds me of the poster issued by Christian Aid some years ago, which said 'Ignore the hungry and they will go away—to their graves'. If we eliminate all the severely affected children with spina bifida there will be no more problem; but why stop at spina bifida, why not all the severely affected spastics, all those with muscular dystrophy, and those with Down's syndrome? Why stop at the neonatal period?[4]

These views are typical of almost the entire pro-life lobby. In practice, however, the matter is more complicated. Mothers suffer great pain and agony when they give birth to a deformed child. Modern science has now given doctors the ability to forecast the likelihood of certain disabilities. It therefore follows that affected mothers must suffer a terrible mental agony whilst carrying the child, thus endangering their psychological health. What this means is that both grounds for abortion have merged into one another. It is possible to argue quite compassionately that those willing to carry out a eugenic abortion are not seeking to eliminate disability, but to improve the mental health and probably the physical health of the mother concerned. Such an argument helped to sway the General Assembly of the Church of Scotland in 1986 to return to a more liberal position on abortion. It is important to note that the wording of the Act now becomes even more blurred than it was in previous times. It is insufficient to say that a woman should be able to face up to the knowledge that she is carrying a potentially disabled child, when in reality the courage required to do so is beyond all but the strongest, and the area of choice left to the mother is emotionally restricted.

There are of course the feelings of disabled people to be considered. The general consensus is that if a disabled person admits that eugenic abortion is justifiable, he is thereby undermining the value of his own life. Victims of spina bifida appear to be particularly prominent in pro-life organisations recognising the precarious way in which they as individuals are valued by society. Adequate care and understanding can give the victims of spina bifida a very good life. With the aid of calipers, they can learn to walk; surgery can overcome the effects of an open lesion; hydrocephalus and the incontinence which will be with them throughout their lives can be treated with many different kinds of surgical aids from a very early age. The neonatal stage is of supreme importance because it is at this stage of life that surgery can promote a high quality of living in later years, and also, and perhaps more importantly, save life.[5] There is also great concern about screening.

There is considerable strain imposed on any mother who undergoes these tests. Although earlier tests are being developed, the amniocentesis comes at a fairly late stage in pregnancy and threatens to reveal to the mother that the child she most dearly wants is disabled. It would take great resolve to overcome the trauma of a positive result. Tests are both a means of relieving anxiety and yet increasing it. Some mothers are relieved that they can continue assured of a happy pregnancy, whilst others have to choose between having an abortion or accepting a new and unplanned lifestyle.

Professor J K Mason of the University of Edinburgh has pointed out that several cases have been raised claiming damages for wrongful genetic counselling. So far the courts have refused to grant damages to parents aggrieved by the birth of a disabled child after contrary advice.

Pro-life groups tend to have handicapped sections which take a very positive and dogmatic stance against any research which threatens life. Typical is the opinion of one writer in the 1985 Spring issue of the Newsletter of the Society for the Protection of the Unborn Child (Handicapped Division): 'We must make it quite clear that while of course we would prefer not to be handicapped, we cannot and will not allow other human beings to be used and destroyed in the name of pre-venting our disabilities'.

Such attitudes have led to divisions of opinion regarding research. To be most efficiently carried out, research always requires a control group. In perinatal care this may involve putting some mothers at an unknown risk. Such research is of course scrutinised by ethical committees and some has been modified to a more acceptable standard. Nevertheless it is clear that the Society for the Protection of the Unborn Child does not consider it to be ethically justifiable to cause any risk or to deny any treatment to a control group which might result in the loss of a fetus. This puts them in conflict with a lot of research and with the scientific or medical community as a whole. It means that they oppose research into the most effective forms of screening and into the use of drugs to lessen the risk of the development of spina bifida and other congenital deformities. This sort of religious discourse is not amenable to scientific method. On the other hand, scientific methodology is the province of a community of which the majority of the public are not members.

There is also, of course, vehement opposition to the pro-posals put forward by the Warnock Report, which recom-mends that research be permitted to be carried out on 'spare' embryos until the fourteenth day of development. The Warnock Committee considers it safe to go to the fourteenth day because it is only after this that the first neural tissue appears, and also because implantation in the womb does not take place until around this time. The research envisaged, it has been suggested, might lead to a better understanding of the causes not only of infertility, but also of conditions such as spina bifida and Down's syndrome. Others have gone so far as

to suggest that the research might develop into an understanding of the origins of cystic fybrosis and muscular dystrophy, for example; and, if we take our research a stage
further, genetic engineering might eliminate diseases such as
haemophilia.[6] While understanding the anxiety and the high
motives of those who will not countenance research which
endangers the unborn child, I feel that their position is too
narrow and conservative.

An alternative position is thus necessary. Since I consider
that a disabled person is only complete when accepted and
loved by others, so I adhere to the position that the embryo
can only be accorded the status of life when it becomes viable.
Inevitably this will mean that as technology improves, the
stage up to which a fetus may be aborted will become earlier.
As a rule I do not believe that life really takes on any human
characteristics prior to the stage when it has the human
potential to be part of society. In other words, parents must
be conscious that they have successfully conceived, and then,
several weeks later, they must be aware that their fetus could
be considered viable. Within these parameters it is normally
correct to allow restricted research, and also to consider
screening with a view to termination.

Such a definition will not satisfy the disabled people and the
pro-life groups which have been mentioned. But they must
attempt to find another way of regarding themselves in order
to gain a radically different self-image. From a Christian
point of view they must find the faith to cope with the new
technology, and they must also develop a self-image which
allows them to live securely in a world of change.

Dorothee Sölle argues that with Christ the trials of Job
came to an end.[7] Man no longer has to suffer the puzzling
injustice of God because God himself has suffered on the
cross for us. In so doing he has shown how we can take
responsibility for our own lives for the good of society. We
can begin to explore how the individual becomes part of that
society, and then begin to challenge that individual to accept a
rôle working to the glory of God in Jesus Christ. In casual
documents for pro-life groups we read words like 'frightened',
and judgmental words like 'murder' or 'holocaust'. We should
be looking rather for words which express the compassion

which gynaecologists and others have for those who are going to suffer more deeply. We must also ensure that our society is such that the disabled person can feel certain that his life, his rôle, is valued; that his parent's efforts to make him a useful member of society are deeply appreciated, and that his life is in no way under valued by the fact that we wish to eradicate the conditions from which he suffers.

Such an attitude is, of course, open to the charge of being too liberal. We cannot as Christians afford to be careless over human life, and we must seek to put limits upon our desires to solve our problems through eugenic abortions. Parents have the right to choose, and this right is particularly important to women. Society, however, has failed to point out the number of choices which can be made. These choices are all present in pro-life literature, but they do not appear to be spelled out clearly enough with an unequivocal meaning. *First*, parents can choose not to have children if they feel that they are at risk. It might be possible to eliminate Huntingdon's Chorea within a generation if such attempts were made by many carriers. Others may be compelled by reading the signs after a difficult first pregnancy, or they may know that they have received genetic counselling advising them against a child. *Second*, mothers may refuse to undergo screening. *Third*, they have a choice in rejecting the indicators of such tests. Both these latter choices are difficult to make. The medical profession has more or less put great pressure on most parents to accept the offer of screening and to agree to abide by the findings, yet nevertheless they should allow choice to be made in this delicate area. *Fourth*, consequent upon the previous two points, the mother may decide that she wishes to carry a disabled child. *Fifth*, and we must note how low it is in our rankings, parents may choose to terminate a pregnancy.

Those disabled people who feel very strongly that it is their duty to campaign for a more responsible attitude have all these choices to advocate. They can build greater respect for their own lives by drawing out the very real possibilities that parents have when they consider raising a family, and they can point out to society that it too has obligations. Society must foster a more responsible attitude, and it must also be aware that our government does not adequately cater for those who are going to be born with a congenital handicap. Insufficient provision has been made available for perinatal care and little thought has been given to the actual cost of providing the services necessary to offer a real quality of life to those who are born with a disability. If our society is to become compassionate, it must prove itself willing to pay for the care of those handicapped people who are being given life by their parents' choice. Society must be positive in funding care rather than negative in eliminating the need for care. Urgent need for sufficient funding is something which neither the Church nor the Government has faced up to. Ironically both are held back by dogma. The Church exhibits conservative dogma held very sincerely and correctly within a certain theological framework, but it must be prepared to pay the price of such adherence. Likewise the government in its 'free-market' dogma must learn that care at this level might possibly be as costly as the defence of the realm which it is only too willing to support.

The Report on abortion to the General Assembly of 1987 has been awaited with great expectation. It wisely conceded that there were differences of opinion which had to be respected. There were divided opinions over fetal deformity and abortion. It argued, on the one hand, that disabled children were to be valued and granted their place in eternity; whilst on the other, it recognised the agony which parents often suffer. The Revd John Stevenson, in presenting the Report, expressed the hope that the Church could 'speak with one voice, [that] it will do so, and where it cannot that it will still allow different voices to be heard with grace and understanding'.

When the Bible is placed in our hands as members of the Church, and as believers in Jesus Christ, we are given one of the most powerful and persuasive books ever written. We believe that it contains the Rule of Life, and would expect it to guide our actions in most spheres of our life. The Bible can be read and received as a book of literal authority. It can be read as a literary work concerned with a Third World type society, and with issues which were apparent and could be solved in small nomadic or simple urban communities. These communities were not complicated by great technology nor any political complexities beyond the corruption of kings. To apply this book literally to the problem facing the disabled, and in particular to those who are congenitally disabled, is to misuse it. What we do receive is access to the grace of God through the spirit of his Son Jesus Christ. After we have received this spirit we are guided into all truth and given a maturity in which to make decisions regarding the quality of our life and the nature of our society. The Spirit of Christ, both pre-existent in the Old Testament and amidst the people in the New, shows quite clearly that Christ had great sympathy for the disabled. Other passages show the sympathy he had for those who suffered remorse, or suffered persecution. There seems little doubt that if we pray for guidance under the grace of God, we will be given a maturity and an understanding to continue to accept and welcome the disabled child in our midst, and watch him develop as his growth in society continues.

It is not that there is no biblical solution or explanation for disability, it is rather that we must look to Christ and his way as interpreted by the Church in order to find it. There is, however, an intermediate stage. In this stage we find that the disabled are regarded as people who display a quality of life which is worthy of admiration and of support.

Notes to Chapter 2

1   A Weiser, *The Psalms* (Old Testament Library Series) (SCM Press, London, 1979)
2   C R Fradd, 'An Introduction to the History and Present State of the Law Relating to Abortion in England' from *Abortion and the Sanctity of Human Life* (edited by J H Channer) (The Paternoster Press, Exeter, 1985)
3   C R Fradd, *ibid*
4   R B Zachery, 'Life with Spina Bifida' from *British Medical Journal* (1977)
5   R B Zachery, *ibid*
6   Dame Mary Warnock, *Report of the Committee of Inquiry into Human Fertilization and Embryology* (HMSO, London, 1984), ch 11
7   Dorothee Sölle, *Suffering* (Darton, Longman and Todd, London, 1975), p 119 ff

3

Disability and Public Sentiment

The British are both compassionate and sentimental. They are alleged to be concerned about cruelty to animals, less so about cruelty to children and even less about the plight of the elderly. They have proved to successive governments that they are willing to give more aid to Third World countries than the governments themselves. They have a notable and insatiable appetite for publicity showing the success and the struggle of those who seek to come to terms with disability. The concern of television with the disabled is best observed by looking at television coverage which has produced many documentaries which in actual fact often border on voyeurism.

Some of these documentaries have been so good that they are now available on general release from the charities most involved. Perhaps the most touching and certainly the most moving was the film 'Like Other People', produced in 1972 and televised as one of the 'Man Alive' series. It depicted the love and subsequent marriage of two severely spastic people who lived in a residential home. After being seen on television, this film had somewhat the same impact as the documentary 'Cathy Come Home' had for the homeless. It altered the entire attitude of disabled people and their carers to sex and marriage. Another documentary—'Joey'—told the tale of an individual's struggle; 'The Visit' portrayed the determined struggle of a plastic surgeon to rebuild the face of a very deformed boy from South America whom he and his wife later adopted; and regional programmes have witnessed the care which is lavished on some brain damaged children. Much of the television coverage is excellent and one of Britain's soap operas, 'Crossroads', shows how attitudes are maturing. Many years ago there was a character named

Sandy who was in a wheelchair and suffered the indignity of every cliché that could be written about him. In 1986 'Crossroads' was actually persuaded to have a Down's syndrome child on the programme in order that the problems of adoption, fostering and community care could be discussed in a popular way. Both BBC and ITV have regular programmes of information, but the News programmes, however, tend to highlight spectacular occurrences, giving a very distorted understanding of disability at peak viewing times.

In recent years documentaries have tended to become individualistic, focussing on one family's search for treatment, and often treatment which has sometimes been assumed to be only available outside Britain. Lately, for example, the media has been concerned with a new treatment for cerebral palsy considered to be unique but not available in Britain. In fact Westerlea School in Edinburgh was using the Hungarian techniques in modified forms 30 years ago. (See Introduction.) All of the documentaries, however, depict a determination on the part of the parents of a disabled person to overcome the disability which has crippled their family life and demanded so much of their time. Some documentaries have been occasioned by legal judgments which have had some effect upon the life of those concerned. Without fail they demonstrate the determination and seeming courage of parents and children, or disabled adults alike. However, the dramatised documentary, 'Joey', the story of a spastic from childhood through to adulthood in a mental hospital is so outstandingly good compared to some more recent works. This film shows starkly the effect of inadequate treatment of cerebral palsy when a man such as Joey was a child. The inexperienced viewer often extracts the wrong message from these films! Most people thought that this film was a reflection on mental hospitals whereas it was really a comment on a physical condition which had been little understood and largely ignored in the days of Joey's childhood.

It is, however, in the run of the mill television productions that we see most starkly two different attitudes to disability portrayed on television. We have, on the one hand, a syndrome which has not thus far been named; this we might call the 'Songs of Praise syndrome'. In Songs of Praise, five or six people are asked to choose a hymn and to explain why they have chosen it. Very often on that programme there is an opportunity for one disabled person to appear as a source of inspiration. In this situation the disabled person is almost a 'statutory inclusion', singled out because of the qualities he or she can exhibit to others which can do little else but inspire in the few minutes made available. On the other hand, we have a type of programme which treats the disabled person in a perfectly normal matter of fact way. In this country we have on BBC television a sports programme for children which always includes a number in the series for disabled pupils. This programme is entitled 'We are the Champions', and shows the disabled as they are and as their capabilities allow. Similarly, there is 'Sesame Street' from America, which integrates children with Down's syndrome or spastic children into the play and activities of normal children. These programmes do not overtly offer a message, but they may discomfort many who watch because the disabled are being portrayed in their natural context without a 'message' behind it. The contrast between programmes which present a 'message' (such as 'Songs of Praise') and those which integrate disabled people, is symptomatic, perhaps even pathologically so, of society's views of the sufferer and the spectator. The former benefits the spectator, the latter the sufferer.

I remember an incident which to this day reminds me of the gulf which can exist between the spectator, disabled people and their helpers. A group of spastics were once out on a day trip and, if my memory serves me right, were bored. A lady came up and offered to buy them ice cream and on parting said, 'I suppose they're happy *in their own way*'. The lady was inwardly saying that she felt reassured that these spastics were being offered a quality of life which justified their existence and satisfied her need to contribute to their happiness. The fact that her comment was scorned and laughed at by the spastics and their helpers only demonstrates that the problem before us is much more acute, and almost pathetic.

The Search for a Reason for Living

It is perhaps not without coincidence that Britain has produced philosophers concerned with ideas about happiness. Often there is a desperate search for a quality of life to offer disabled people. This offer is genuine but it can be impeded by the inertia of public opinion which is only slowly seeking to undo the damaging and handicapping effects of social discrimination.

The teleological argument has been raised in some way or another by most of the Church Fathers. Aquinas argued that, 'Some intelligent being exists by whom all natural things are directed to their end; and this we call God'.[1] Augustine was concerned with another dimension of the argument when he wrote, 'Since God is the highest good, He would not allow any evils to exist in His works, unless His omnipotence and goodness were such as to bring good even out of evil'.[2] The argument, basically, is that God so created the world that his creation is working towards an end which is good, and therefore the design of the world is such that God's hand must be seen at work in it even when evil occurs. God is also seen as an architect: the perfect design of nature is the product of his almighty mind, and his existence is surely proved by the way in which nature moves towards an end. David Hume, the Scottish philosopher, pointed out the fact that observing the work of an architect does nothing more than to prove that a clever designer is present. Likewise he argued that if people found a clock in a deserted spot, they could either conclude that the clock was the product of a superb clockmaker or that by some random probability the mechanism had come together. It therefore does not seem as if an argument from design necessarily proves the existence of God, but it certainly has the profound effect of compelling Christians to justify seeming defects in the 'grand design'.

In order to judge the quality of life we must look at the whole of it. Later in this chapter we shall see that many legal judgments are based on nursing care and material comfort. In practice, life is compartmentalised and dealt with at different levels, and by different disciplines. Speech therapists look for good communication, teachers for a high academic achievement, and medical practitioners for less pain and the maximum output from the body. Sometimes doctors are very good at treating medical symptoms but fail to understand disability. Many Christians will seek to define the quality of life holistically and would go on to justify it with reference to the 'grand design' of God.

Margaret B Davidson, in her book *You Tell Me*, interviewed 96 spastic adults and included in her questionnaire and interviews material about their religious beliefs. These evoked both negative and positive responses; on the one hand, a number held atheistic viewpoints which were well thought out and showed how attractive atheism can be. (I would suspect that the Church is not especially relevant to disabled people and that sometimes their upbringing encourages a lack of belief.) The easiest way, it seemed, to find a purpose in life and to be reassured of the quality of life was to neglect to answer the very questions which posed problems. On the other hand, those who were positively in favour of Christianity showed great satisfaction in their acceptance by the Christian community; some enjoyed the quietness and serenity of contemplation whilst others offered evidence of an evangelical zeal.[3]

There have of course been many evangelical books written about the triumph of the individual over the suffering which an accident has imposed upon them. The most famous book of this type is *Joni*, an autobiography by Joni Eareckson.[4] An English equivalent to this American publication is *Halfway To Heaven* which tells the story of Max Sinclair.[5] These books have moved many people and it is not hard to realise why. A spinal injury is a traumatic experience both for the body and the psyche. It is said by many that such injuries are usually sustained by active successful people, and this was certainly true of these two writers. The way in which they describe the shock of their accidents is most moving. In a matter of hours they feel that they regress physically from adulthood to infancy. They are stripped of all dignity and left totally dependent on others for every task; the movement of even a finger is a cause for celebration. Both these authors came from a religious background: Joni's family was typical of affluent middle class American church families, whilst Max was himself a full time evangelist. After the initial shock of their accidents, the compelling motive behind their writing was to bring good out of evil. They were surely aware of the verse in Romans:

> We know that in all things God works for good with those who love him, those whom he has called according to his purpose.
> (Rom. 8:28)

These writers stress in their books their constant need to pray and attend to God's word. Max very soon finds his ministry in showing his love of God within the wards of Stoke Mandeville Hospital and within his own Christian community. At a later stage, with more maturity, he ministers most movingly to his young daughter:

> And God again used the words of a child to remind me when that miracle would be perfected. We were round an evening fire at home, Annie on my knee and Noddy at my feet, and Ben nearly asleep in Sue's arms.
> 'If I'm naughty, you can't run after me and catch me,' Annie was telling me gleefully.
> Noddy looked up. 'In heaven,' she said seriously, as if there was something Annie had overlooked, 'Daddy will get a new pair of legs.'
> 'Oh dear.' Annie put her finger in her mouth and her other arm round my neck. 'Well I better be a good girl in heaven then.'[6]

In a brief anecdote, Sinclair has summed up the teleological arguments. Everything will be perfected, but only in heaven, which is not characteristic of the argument of this book.

The significant point of such literature is the conviction of the writers that God directs not only the course of recovery but the way in which a new meaning in life can be found. There is a considerable thankfulness for God's guidance to the new state of awareness and grace. The authors almost become grateful for the insights their accidents have given them.

This, Dorothee Sölle introduces as the concept of Christian masochism in her analysis of suffering. She quotes a prayer from Luther not dissimilar to this English one:

'O give us patience and steadfastness in adversity, strengthen
our weakness, comfort us in trouble and distress, help us to
fight; grant unto us that in true obedience and contention of
mind we may give over our own wills unto thee our Father in
all things, according to the example of thy beloved Son; that in
adversity we grudge not, but offer up ourselves unto thee
without contradiction.... O give us a willing and cheerful
mind, that we may gladly suffer and bear all things for thy
sake.'

(Bishop Miles Coverdale, 1488–1568)[7]

Sölle argues that there is almost a compulsive desire on the
part of Christians to suffer; and by so doing to produce good.
We find old people who are going deaf describing in religious
magazines not only the difficulties but the compensations: the
marvels of hearing aids, of teletext sub-titles; of churches
fitted with the conduction loop system. These are compensations indeed, but do they deserve to become virtues?

Mothers who have just discovered that their child is disabled are reassured that their child will respond to them with
a love and affection deeper than most. As their relationship
develops they may well begin to feel that the child is here for a
purpose. Often when a child, disabled or not, dies at a young
age, God's purpose in allowing that death can be inappropri-
ately described in such terms as 'God wanted another flower
in his garden'. Similar words can be found in many newspaper *In Memoriam* notices. These forms of mourning over a
death, the onset of old age, loss of mobility, hearing, sight,
and so on, are understandable and sometimes very moving in
a household where there is limited understanding and a deep
devotion, but they do not really progress to a stage of adjust-
ment and acceptance. Christian masochism demands that we
do not seek to ameliorate our situation but that we simply
acquiesce in submission to God's will. If we are prepared to be
angry and resentful with other people, surely we may also be
angry with God and rage at our misfortune which we deem is
not part of his design.

Disabled people now have a high profile, albeit a sometimes
ineffective one. Gone are the days when they were shut away
and not talked of. Joey's misfortune affects less and less
people: the media, the public and the Church have done as

much as they can to offer disabled people a status. Yet the problem remains that all publicity and encouragement are geared towards what I believe to be an outdated paradigm of the triumph of virtue over the depths of despair, lack of attention and misfortune. Society must move towards a radical acceptance of the recognition of disabled people's rights which allows them to take an equal place in society. As long as there is pity, an inflated admiration, or a desire that disabled people should not express their true feelings, there will not be an amelioration of their situation. The shocking thing to both disabled and non-disabled people in the film 'Like Other People', for example, was the frankness with which the couple shared their feelings. Similarly, within the Church, only a theology which liberates will be able to cope with a heightened awareness of disabled people's frustration and anger expressed with a frankness which is not part of Christian masochism.

Indeed, outside the Church and religious discourse, anger has done more to alter the quality of life for the disabled when its creative power has been changed or has invoked law for the benefit of the disabled. There is also an alternative both to anger and to pietistic acceptance which we will discuss after consideration of the way society defines the 'quality of life', and the institutional mechanisms by which attempts are made to achieve it.

Disability and the Legal Process

All law directly or indirectly emanates from the realm of politics. Every political party in this country makes the welfare of the disabled a major item in its manifesto. Countless polls have shown that while these items are very low in the voters' list of priorities, leading politicians must be seen to be caring. Public opinion has forced successive governments to alter and improve the law, thus giving us a ready reckoner of the value and quality of life which society will be prepared to offer the disabled. In the last chapter it was apparent that the law on abortion was considered negatively as a law which denied quality of life. In the corpus of law to be considered in this chapter, in contrast, there is a positive response by all. Apart from minor technicalities and certain external influences such as the European Court of Justice, there is very little which disrupts the consensus amongst the influence makers.

It is convenient to divide the law into three categories: *first*, the statutory provisions for the disabled which are really dealt with adequately in many other books; *second*, the damages awarded to disabled people mostly by civil judgments; and *third*, legal discourse about future developments.

It is almost 27 years since medical science was responsible for the Thalidomide tragedy. Even now there are legal actions being taken over a similar drug called Debendox. In England and Wales there are two Acts which protect the unborn child against injury. These Acts, the Infant Life Preservation Act 1929 and the Congenital Disabilities (Civil Liability) Act 1976, offer protection and compensation for injury caused through the negligence of some third person. The ability to sue and receive compensation gives parents a measure of the value to be placed on the quality of their child's life. In this country we saw evidence of low compensation when in 1986 some Scottish parents won the right to sue the makers of Debendox in the American courts which were likely to offer much higher levels of compensation. Again the British Government has offered low rates of compensation for whooping cough vaccination damage to infants. These rates have been challenged in the courts since parents obviously have found it hard to accept the quality of life offered.

In the realm of medical accidents, we find some interesting judgments which tell us much about the courts' attitudes to quality of life. A notable case involved a doctor who suffered a cardiac arrest and irreparable brain damage after a minor gynaecological operation in 1973.[8] She had a promising career ahead of her and could reasonably have expected to become a consultant psychiatrist. She was awarded record damages of £254 765; the case went to an appeal in the House of Lords where her damages were sustained, but not without some dissension. The interest in this case is two-fold. *First*, Lord Denning's comments in the Court of Appeal are of relevance, and *second* it illustrates how damages are assessed.

Lord Denning gave a very important judgment in which he stated some matters of principle. He considered that the main grounds for damages were to award the woman a sufficient sum to keep her comfortable for the rest of her life. He argued that since she could no longer dispose of funds because of her lack of mental ability she had no need for all the other elements in excess of nursing care. He then went on to argue that he was faced with a peculiarly modern moral problem. In the past, medicine would not have saved her life and the pressure to seek high levels of compensation was greater as a consequence from relatives who wished to keep her alive. There have been attempts to limit the amount of compensation in cases where most of the quality of life has been destroyed. Finally, Lord Denning argued that it would be undesirable to waste public money raising levels of insurance and of liability for medical malpractice. Unlike the United States, this country could not afford to pay huge sums on litigation and compensation at the expense of the taxpayer. Lord Denning's arguments have implications far beyond this case.

Briefly, however, it is interesting to note how damages are assessed. There are elements for loss of present earnings, cost of care, loss of future earnings and of pension rights and, last, damages for pain and suffering. Lord Denning's remarks begged many questions. Cases such as these have to be paid out of the public purse, which is a limited fund. How much can we afford to spend in valuing quality of life? The debate is not now about eugenics, but about the value we place upon lives of victims of mishaps over which we have no control. Should we limit by statute the amount of compensation payable? The lady doctor in this case had no direct dependants and it was proposed that she should therefore receive less than a married person with children. Is there a real difference in quality of life between one who has a family and one who has not? All of these questions must be asked and reasonably answered. What they appear to be saying is that it is exceedingly difficult for the legal system to 'price' a quality of life. Circumstances vary so very much that it would be attractive to judges to have regular guidelines and maximum awards, as Lord Denning suggested. But it is precisely in the case of vaccine damages that regular amounts have been rejected, mainly because of the paucity of the award. The temptation to sue for higher amounts is a measure of people's search for quality, but there is yet another inconsistency.

The public responds in different ways to different events. The disabling of a policeman, or a soldier in the Falklands campaign for instance, attracts a great deal of money from public donations. So does the individual 'miracle cure' which is only available in another country. There is a stark contrast between the individual affected and his family who often benefit enormously from a traumatic accident; and the happy prosperous family who suddenly have to cope with multiple sclerosis, a stroke, or a similar disabling disease which strikes unexpectedly and often affecting the breadwinner of the family. (Strokes are not in fact confined to the elderly.) It would appear in the matter of Civil Law, that we do not have any guidance to the quality of life but only an *ad hoc* way of relieving certain circumstances. In fact, the law and public sentiment appear to perpetuate and increase inequalities in the way disabled people live.

In early 1982 the Department of Health and Social Security (DHSS) published the Report by the Committee on Restrictions Against Disabled People (CORAD). This is perhaps the most important Report since the International Year of the Disabled Person (IYDP); reference will be made to it again in a later chapter. The Report devotes a chapter to possible future legislation which would make discrimination on the grounds of disability illegal. Such legislation would be different from the type already discussed in that it would be declaratory and educative. The Committee reached their conclusions after an examination of foreign experience. The Rehabilitation Act (1973) forced American employers to make every attempt to employ disabled people. Section 504 requires that:

> No otherwise qualified handicapped individual in the United States ... shall, solely by reason of his handicap, be excluded from participating in, be denied the benefits of, or be subjected to discrimination under any programme or activity receiving Federal financial assistance.[9]

This legislation was greeted with a great deal of enthusiasm, but many mistakes were made which almost made the beneficiaries unpopular. The 'Davis case' went to the Supreme Court which sensibly decided that a woman with a serious hearing loss did not have an unqualified right to enter nursing college. Canada's legislation is slightly weaker, whilst in Australia legislation affecting disabled people has generally been subsumed under anti-discrimination legislation.

In Britain there is legislation protecting the rights of disabled people. Most of these laws are enforced by voluntary compliance, but the Committee reached the conclusion that there was now a case for enforceable anti-discrimination legislation.

The Committee was reluctant to make such a recommendation, *first* because of the difficulty of defining 'disabled', *second* because of the costs, and *third* because educative legislation is not noticeably successful. It has taken years to persuade people to wear seat belts, and the Commission on Racial Equality or the Equal Opportunities Commission have not enjoyed great success in their aims either.

A minority report, not dissimilar to the attitude of many churchmen, argued that legislation would set disabled people apart and harden attitudes.[10] On balance, however, it was considered that legislation was necessary, but it would appear that no government, present or future, has accepted the need to implement such legislation.

What would such legislation achieve? It would insist that a disabled person would be considered equally when applying for a job, course, or facility; that an accurate medical assessment would have to be made, and that any compensation grants or aids from the government would have to be considered (for instance, the government offers upwards of £6000 to an employer to adapt a place of work). The public would be protected from the possibility of disabled people being an actual danger in a situation, and from unreasonable expense and embarrassment when there is no practical way of accommodating a disabled person.

The two recommendations are:

(1) The Law should cover all areas where discrimination occurs, and particularly employment, education, the provision of goods, facilities and services, insurance, transport, property rights, occupational pension schemes, membership of associations and clubs, and civic duties and functions.

(2) There should be a regulatory body or Commission with powers to investigate, conciliate and if necessary take legal action on individual complaints of discrimination; to recommend guidelines on the reasonable affirmative action required to accommodate disabled people and to promote the integration of disabled people into society.[11]

Such legislation would confer rights, and place before the public an agenda for the acceptance of the disabled. The Church has an uneasy relationship with present Equal Opportunities legislation. For instance, it is allowed to discriminate against women on the grounds of doctrine in favour of denominational interests, if it considers that it should employ a person of a particular denomination. Since the Church has no doctrinal objection to disabled people, it would have to take seriously the agenda written in list (1) and enter unreservedly into any new legislation.

There is, however, one further type of legislation, other than educative, which involves human rights. British jurists have always argued successfully that the supremacy of Parliament is a better and more flexible guardian than a written Constitution. The latter would be both declaratory and enforceable, and is becoming much more acceptable in British society under champions such as Lord Hailsham. He and many others believe that Britain now requires a Constitution to mark the aims of our society, and to demarcate the limits of legislation. The United Kingdom is not subject to any such Declarations or Treaties in ways which are legally binding. It has not yet ratified the United Nations Declaration on the Rights of Disabled Persons (1975). Our membership of the Common Market, however, has bound us much more to treaties and codes, and these are enforceable through the European Court. What we see developing now is a pressure to recognise human rights and to reject laws which discriminate.

Scandinavian countries already have laws which provide rights for their citizens, which have been successfully conferred upon the disabled. CORAD comments favourably on the requirement that Swedish newspapers produce cassette versions for blind people at no extra charge—not because they are blind, but because their blindness inhibits their constitutional right to freedom of information.[12] Civic rights would be considered in CORAD's proposals for legislation. Why should disabled people be barred from jury service or from high civic office by discrimination or convenience?

In July 1986 the Government accepted a ruling of the European Court in a case brought by Mrs Jacqueline Drake seeking payment of an invalid care allowance for married women who are classed as 'carers'. Governments have always accepted that chronic invalids are better cared for at home than in institutions. It has always been assumed that Governments could depend upon the goodwill of married daughters to give up work opportunities to look after dependent relatives. The European Court's judgment has clearly put an end to sex discrimination and also to the Government's exploitation of family love and goodwill.[13] Our legislators are being brought into a new realm where rights matter and *ad hoc* payments to various bodies concerned with community care are simply not enough. As we go on to discuss charities we can see that the present Government's list of financial support to bodies concerned with 'carers' is described by the Opposition as a 'joke'.[14] This country will learn that respect for basic rights is bound to be costly and it is necessary to meet the financial needs of 70 000 women who can claim £29 per week for Invalid Care Allowance. This advance in human rights alone may cost the British taxpayer £55 million per year.

I have chosen to dwell at length on the legal process because it is too easy to talk of affording a quality of life without defining it. The law at least does this. The award of damages not only puts a price on an individual's life, but signals pressure for reform. Discrimination humiliates every disabled person at some time and so their frustrations ought to be channelled into reforms. Dignity can be conferred by human rights. Perhaps the disabled should not be treated as 'unfortunate accidents' but should be offered the opportunity of taking an equal place in a progressive society. In order to achieve this, they and their relatives must come together. This they do already through charities, but not all of their problems are solved in the many hours of unselfish giving which go into the efforts of the thousands of charities working for their welfare.

Charity and Disability

Charities have become much more politicised over the last ten years and, as a result of Government fiscal policy, they have both benefited and suffered. They have suffered at the hands of local authorities cutting back and by national Governments' successive budgets which at a stroke can reduce allocations to charities. Nevertheless, they have benefited from more liberal covenant schemes and the new emphasis on commercial sponsorship. It is difficult to say whether charities for disabled people have more or less opportunity today. But there is definitely a conscious objective in Government policy to allow the charities to develop ways of enhancing the quality of life of their members. Every referral agency, including Church ministers, should possess a copy of the *Directory for Disabled People* published by the Royal Association for Disability and Rehabilitation (known as RADAR).

I have little reason to believe that the story of the origins of charities has changed much in my lifetime. Parents of disabled people have a strong sense of isolation when confronted by disability. They search for people in similar circumstances and club together to share their experiences and merge resources. It is moving to read the list of private addresses from which some such support groups have emanated. Within the walls of that house a plea for help has at some time been uttered; and it has been answered, not so much by the immediate help that is offered, but by the companionship that is engendered. We are tempted to think that charity is mainly about fund raising. Whilst not belittling the need for money, it is the need for support and encouragement which is most important in charities for disabled people and their relatives. Such may be said of charities which seek to provide an understanding of a particular condition. But there is also a second group of charities which provide activities for disabled people and recognise their need to enter every sphere of life. Thus we have international paraplegic games, riding for the disabled, talking books, and a host of other schemes, including a number of Christian fellowships which are listed in the Directory. Many victims of spinal injury have been very active prior to their accident and 'activity' charities offer them the opportunity of adventure which they have lost. One most unusual charity provides ski-ing for paraplegics, who can come hurtling down the ski slopes in their adapted wheelchairs.

All of these charities have the opportunity of affiliating with umbrella organisations such as RADAR or the Scottish Council for Disability. Many of these fragmented charities enjoy the support of the larger, more well known organisations. Look at any of the annual reports of the large charitable organisations and one will find countless affiliated bodies representing the small groups of people who support one another in more intimate ways than the larger bodies can do.

It is at the level of national charities that disabled people have to be presented to the public. This takes us back from the realm of private personal support, to the problem of the spectator and the sufferer. Most major organisations offer some kind of award to some disabled person each year. These afford much publicity and influence the way in which the public see disabled people. We have, for instance, the Disabled Scot of the Year; RADAR offers a number of awards; and a women's magazine presents the annual recognition of 'Children of Courage', some of whom are disabled. The theme of courage or special achievement runs through many of these awards and offers an easy solution to one of the problems which is central to this chapter: What is God's purpose for the disabled? Is it to inspire and encourage others?

Margaret Davidson was apprehensive when she first went to teach spastic children. She confessed to just an average knowledge of disability, yet over the years she came to be relaxed with spastic adults. During her reported conversations, she came to see that 'courage' was not the right word to use, but that 'resilience' characterised their approach to life more accurately.[15] It was in part my own comments that led her to this conclusion, and so we must expand it a little.

The process of handicapped living is such that there is a constant need for adaptation. A great many disabled people hold down difficult jobs which to the spectator are already difficult but seem to be impossible in the light of disability. The disabled person learns to adapt the circumstances of a career in such a way that the spectator is not always aware of just how complicated these adaptations are. They are almost 'trade secrets'.

Simon Weston was a soldier who suffered multiple burns in the Falklands. His dexterity is impeded by the burns to his hands and his social integration is handicapped by the gross disfigurement of his face. His progress from injury to recovery was well documented on BBC television and allows us to separate possible descriptions of his character. That he was physically courageous is beyond doubt. This kind of courage has inspired and will do so to the end of time, but it has little to do with the eventual disability. Recovery from an injury or corrective surgery of any type can be very painful and very demanding. Anyone who successfully undergoes such treatment can show a tremendous courage which has nothing to do with the disability they have or will have. The medical process which Joni or Max Sinclair or this brave soldier underwent has an inevitability about it which has little to do with the qualities which they will require to live a successful life. 'Resilience' describes the process of ignoring the gasping horror when people see a disfigured face or when they ignore you when you seem to be inferior in a wheelchair. There is perhaps yet another kind of courage. This is the courage which allows the disabled person to share the 'trade secrets', the private matters which allow them to be successful. This type of courage improves the quality of life for others but is not the type which the public perceives. The normal day to day adaptations to people's attitudes, to thinking through the next small adaptation to allow you to do something new, is not 'courageous' but is the normal process of a disabled life which can be so frustrating that only resilience can overcome it.

Thus, charity and its surrounding publicity can be both necessary and unfair. They are necessary in that people need charities to find kindred spirits; and necessary in that charities can win costly benefits for disabled people acting either as pressure groups or fund raisers. Charities, nevertheless, are burdensome in so far as they define in the public mind the lifestyle of disabled people and they give the image of a very high quality of life which it is hard to match in real life.

The public and disabled people alike are forced to accept artificially high standards. It is permissible to discuss the value of a disabled person in terms of their happiness and utilitarian value to those around them, whilst ignoring their innermost feelings. The pain of being deprived of mobility, or the pain of realising in adolescence that life may be more difficult than you optimistically thought, makes one want to reject the values of life which society finds so important. At times happiness can be something that lies in sight of the spectator but is elusive to the disabled person. There must be a Christian explanation for all this excessive or dysteleological suffering.

The Vale of Soul Making

This chapter has attempted to point out that many wish to understand why God allows disability. Most take comfort in the knowledge that their disabled are loved and cared for and given the opportunity in life to develop a degree of comfort and happiness. The public is heartened by the inspiration offered by so many—inspiration that is often channelled through the public relations departments of charities. Parallel to this seeking for comprehension on the part of the public, disabled people are often struggling to get on with life, very successfully. At the same time, the law is seeking to define the aspirations of people very precisely. It does this by the award of damages, reform, or by bringing educative law into the realm of politics. Sometimes all these processes are unfair, more often they tend to reach a sensible conclusion, but now we must try to understand what the process means theologically.

John Hick, in his book *Evil and the God of Love* spends much of his effort discussing teleological theodicies. In his conclusion he develops the concept of a vale of soul making. He argues that suffering is irrational, random, destructive, most of all perhaps, utterly baffling, but that if we understand it right, it can 'contribute to the character of the world as a place in which true human goodness can occur and in which loving and compassionate self-sacrifice can take place'.[16] In Hick's theodicy the world is always working towards an end. God has defined the end in the redemptive work of Jesus Christ. Irenaeus, the second century Bishop of Lyons, believed that mankind would grow more and more into the image of God, and that in Christ we are given the opportunity to take on the new humanity of which St Paul spoke at such length. All Christians can grow into Christ and by so doing become more perfect, yet it would defeat God's purpose to perfect his children by some omnipotent command. Man must rather grow and face up to the randomness of suffering and the temptation of evil which face him as he journeys through the vale which will perfect him. The world's pain is not always evil. A child has to learn that heat signifies danger, that a knife is sharp and can cut, but given respect these dangers can become tremendous, beneficial tools in skilled hands. Hick would argue that even in the natural disasters and pain in the world there can be an ethical dimension. We must account for evil by seeing God's love in Christ rather than by simply looking at God's creative ability in a grand design. Is it the case that all the social processes and all the efforts on the part of individuals to overcome the pain of disability is a moral and good aim in itself; and to reject God because of suffering is to reject his way forward and his actual Divine plan?

The truth of the situation is that disabled people do indeed develop strong well-meaning personalities, and they often have the ability to identify the good things in this world which many others take for granted. These people are not 'unfortunate accidents'; they are part of God's design and the quality of life which we offer is society's recognition expressed in love and compassion. A spastic movement looks tremendously out of place, it even disfigures the body, but we cannot reject the person who is behind the physical movement.

Joni is to be seen not as the victim of an accident, nor as one whose life lost purpose only to be re-discovered as a testimony to Christ; but she must be understood as a triumph of human will over tremendous odds. She sums up the arguments propounded by Hick, probably unwittingly but certainly succinctly, in the following:

'The suffering and pain of the past few years had been the ingredients that had helped me mature emotionally, mentally, and spiritually. I felt confident and independent, trusting in the Lord for my physical and emotional needs. Pain and suffering have purpose. We don't always see this clearly.'[17]

Still, however, a problem remains. Is it at all credible that God is willing to put people through such sufferings in order that they may attain glory in Christ? Several critiques of Hick object to his theodicy, on the basis that suffering almost becomes utilitarian. People who triumph over suffering become 'whole persons'; there is indeed a value according to Hick's argument in watching Joni mature. This I would wish to reject. God cannot be so cruel as actually to cause suffering— in a split second to cause a road accident or a sports accident —so that someone might mature. Of course this objection is slightly too facile because Hick banks on the likelihood that if such victims do not mature in this world they will in the next. Such an evangelical stance is not acceptable to all disabled Christians and is frankly more relevant to evangelicals than to the victims. The brand of evangelism found in Joni is significantly American, whereas most British disabled people are much more sanguine in their beliefs about the influence of God in their life as a disabled person. As in the case of charity, where the public are looking for 'courage' from those who benefit from the charity, so certain churchmen look for a zeal for the Lord which is neither justified nor warranted.

Finally we must ask ourselves whether God's love is limitless. Can he through his Church actually comfort people in the face of such terrible affliction. The answer is 'yes' and 'no'. Positively in the sense that God, once we know what he is about, offers us salvation in Jesus Christ; negatively in the sense that some people simply do not want platitudes about God's love. One cannot be both angry *and* accept Hick's view of God's love.

This chapter has had as an unwritten theme the devotion of many to the betterment of the lives of disabled people. Politicians protest, judges sometimes agonise, charity workers become furious at the public's intransigence, and women like Jacqueline Drake stick their necks out for justice by saying that an appeal to goodwill has gone far enough. Each knows that they are operating in an imperfect system, and if they examine their Christian conscience they realise that God's purpose is hidden in the imperfection. What we must develop is a faith which, whilst explaining, helps us to move forward.

Dorothee Sölle argues that with Christ the necessity for Job disappeared. The Book of Job is not answering the questions Christians ought to be asking. On the cross God himself became the victim. In his helplessness, bearing in his sorrow the lifeless limbs of his Son, he became the paraplegic.[18] God enters into the suffering of the disabled and through his Son redeems them so that they may beat the worst horrors of disability. What we advocate is not the patience of Job, but the zeal of Christ for the wholeness of men and their participation in his ministry of service and of compassion.

Notes to Chapter 3

1   Ninian Smart (editor) *Historical Selections in the Philosophy of Religion* (SCM Press, London, 1962), p 70
2   Ninian Smart (editor), *ibid*
3   Margaret B Davidson, *You Tell Me* (Scottish Council for Spastics, Edinburgh, 1977)
4   Joni Eareckson, *Joni* (Pickering and Inglis, Kent, 1976)
5   Max Sinclair, *Halfway to Heaven* (Hodder & Stoughton, London, 1982)
6   Max Sinclair, *ibid*, p 188
7   *The Oxford Book of Prayer* (Oxford University Press, Oxford)
8   'Lim V Camden Health Authority' from *All England Law Reports*
9   *Report by the Committee on Restrictions Against Disabled People* (CORAD) (Chairman: Mr Peter Large) (DHSS, Crown Copyright, 1982), p 33
10   CORAD, *ibid*, p 73
11   CORAD, *ibid*, p 53
12   CORAD, *ibid*, p 34
13   'Court Confirms Defeat for Government Over "Carers"' (Headline in *The Guardian*, 25 June 1986)
14   'Caring for the Carers' from *Hansard* (no 1134, 1 May 1986)
15   Margaret B Davidson, *op cit*
16   John Hick, *Evil and the Love of God* (Fontana Library, London, 1966), p 372
17   Joni Eareckson, *op cit*, p 159
18   Dorothee Sölle, *Suffering*, p 109 ff

4

A Theology
of Involvement and Identification

Disabled people yearn to be involved in the on-going debates
in the world. Many find within themselves talents which com-
pel them to write, to paint or even to act, in order to express
their acute perception of the world of which they are part.
Many find that their own personal suffering leads them to
think of the needs of others; thus they enter the realms of
political discussion, whilst others are forced, cajoled or willingly take up the cudgels in the cause of their fellow disabled
people. Without intending to return to the issue of abortion,
the following dilemma experienced by Peter McLean illustrates both the perception of people who are disabled and
their awareness of what involvement in the world may imply:

> In view of all the troubles facing the world today (things like
> starvation, the suppression of human rights in many countries
> and the nuclear threat hanging over all of us) I have asked
> myself why should I choose to concentrate on abortion?[1]

There is no answer to Peter's problem. Any answer lies
mainly in factors not connected with one's disability, such as
upbringing, the scope of one's peer group, and even the
nature of one's disability. A spectrum of outside factors can
affect the use of one's talents: the correct form of therapy
may have to be available at the right time and the right place;
Joni, for example, had to be introduced to art; there must
be outlets for writing provided by special schools, or communities, or within the political realm; and one must be able
to enter groups which are open enough to receive disabled
people, and which accept the influence which these people
may have on their policies.

There is overwhelming evidence that the disabled have perceptions which they must share with others and means must be provided for this to be disseminated to the able bodied. The long standing record of the Spastic Society's annual poetry competition judged by Lady Wilson, for example, which has resulted in the book edited by The Spastics Society entitled *Write Angles* which has a foreword by Jeffrey Archer. This amply testifies to the enthusiasm disabled people have for creative writing.

Not far from the inspiration of many is the suffering in the world and of individuals in it. The suffering of the world is now understood by many in the light of the Holocaust. Some disabled people have paid tribute to the one hundred thousand 'undesirables' who were exterminated along with the six million Jews in the concentration camps of the Third Reich. Demonstrators outside the General Assembly of the Church of Scotland did an injustice to the memory of the Holocaust by displaying slogans which, combined with crude visual effects, would turn anyone's stomach: 'The atrocities of the Nazis done in the Name of Christ,' shouted one such demonstrator brandishing a Bible in one hand and a decapitated rubber doll daubed in red paint in the other hand. We do indeed live in a post-Holocaust age and perhaps await the next Holocaust —the Nuclear Holocaust. In such a world there is a great need for people to show that they are involved, a compulsion for them to come to terms with the picture of the world as it *is* today and not as it *ought* to be. Hick's (Irenaean) theodicy may be tidy, but it is subject to the criticism of John K Roth when he reflects that Hick 'sees the world too much as a schoolroom when it is actually more like a dangerous alley'.[2] It is in this world that disabled people plead their cause. Some, with the grace of God, and in response to his love, find an answer to suffering in the cross, in the crucified and risen Christ. This is not always found in biblicism or in a theistic understanding of God's rule of the world.

The image of the cross which concluded the last chapter is not the image which inspires most Christians. Jesus Christ is the Saviour whom God sent to show us the meaning of love in his dealings with his fellow humans. His love was such that he would die in obedience upon the cross and his victory over death would be shown by God in his exaltation of Jesus who is indeed our Saviour. This would show us God's love and doing God's will, in return for which Jesus is now exalted to God's right hand where he intercedes for us. This momentous step in history was made by God so that we might be redeemed; to show that his covenant with the Jews might be turned into a covenant with all mankind spreading outwards. Such a description is neither theological nor poetic, but an accurate summation of many people's beliefs. Jesus showed upon the cross the suffering with which many can identify. He presented to us the image of the perfect summation and a perfect denial of selfishness. This awareness on the part of almost every Christian has led the Church to develop a doctrine of suffering which is not 'masochistic' but almost, as Dorothee Sölle has said, 'sadistic'.[3] The Church offers the people the image of Christ's suffering and proceeds to inflict it upon them.

The temptation of preachers and churchmen is to present a way of suffering which does not involve God in the actual suffering of the individual, but presents him as the Father of the one who shows us how to suffer. The proof text for this preaching can be found in Matthew 10:38: 'Whoever does not take up his cross and follow in my steps is not fit to be my disciple'. Sermons often proclaim that each man and woman has his or her own cross to bear. Such sermons are addressed to those, for example, who suffer from an illness or a marital problem, or often to families having problems caring for delinquent children. Such an attitude to the cross is surely incorrect; indeed it is based on a misunderstanding. The misunderstanding is two-fold. *First*, there is no doubt that the Church has blessed people who bear their crosses nobly, and has offered them a rich reward in heaven. There is probably no possibility of healing in this situation as it exists. Nevertheless, as Francis MacNutt points out, it remains a suffering which is good in particular for the individual and then for the world. The individual can discipline himself and accept the suffering with gladness, but the suffering can also be for the world in as much as people can now see and become inspired by the efforts required to overcome such suffering, to achieve the position of a disciple in taking up the cross of Christ. The paradox is, as MacNutt points out, that Christ released and liberated people from their suffering, rather than binding them to himself through their pain and agony.[4] The Church has succumbed to the temptation of using everyday experience to demonstrate the very unusual suffering of Christ.

Moreover, there is a *second* way of arguing against such a theology. The cross was not something which Christ took up because he had no option. Christ could have walked away from Jerusalem, or he could have defied his Father. The plain truth at the time of his trial led to condemnation which might have been overcome by co-operating with Pilate. The cross Christ bore was borne voluntarily in order to show the love of God. The afflictions which we encounter, however, are forced upon us. We do not enter illness voluntarily, and we go into marriage looking forward to a perfect relationship, and to perfect children. The mishaps of life are random and blind in their injustice to all. They are not examples of God's way of allowing us to participate in the suffering of Christ. The Church must endeavour to dissociate itself from this way of looking at suffering. In this milieu we do not preach to satisfy the needs of the spectator, but rather to give impetus to the life process of those who, through their suffering, have something to offer to society. Society is such that anything that is written by the disabled automatically has the potential of being a source of inspiration, therefore it is likely that no matter which position a disabled person takes, his or her work will be assessed from the presuppositions instilled over centuries by the spectator.

Disabled people can become involved in many different ways, but four are worthy of note. *First*, we have those who by study and application of their experience of themselves find that they become experts on disabled rights. They become involved in secular organisations such as the Disablement Income Group (DIG), or the Disabled Living Foundation (DLF), and many other organisations which are totally separate from the life of the Church. *Second*, there are those people who again are quite secular in their outlook but turn from social policy to politics, recognising the rights of minorities, and the powers invested in the various groups within society. Some of their positions may veer very much to the left, even towards Marxism. Such a body is the Liberation Network of People with Disabilities whose book, *Disabled We Stand*, is representative of their viewpoint. Their position represents a deep political commitment combined with a militant attitude towards their rights which can make the average reader feel guilty when he thinks of his own involvement.

The *third* and *fourth* types of involvement are specifically religious in orientation. For the *third* type, there are those individuals who offer a Christian witness, by relating the stories, the facts of their recovery, and the way in which they have found Christ and through his grace found serenity to live with the new condition. This is the position of Max Sinclair the paraplegic evangelist, and with Joni. There is one such book written by a girl living in Edinburgh who was a member of the congregation of St Giles. Kristine Gibbs develops a similar argument to that of Joni, but does so in the more sanguine manner I spoke of earlier. She almost takes the position of a Nazerite, arguing that she has been spared by God and must give her life to him. In actual fact, her involvement subsequently became more like that of the *first* kind mentioned above through the social work position which she held in Lothian Region.[5] *Fourth*, there is the type of involvement which I now intend to develop, which accepts the disabled person who overcomes his disability, believing in the power of Christ, and through that power finds that he or she can cope with disability and become involved in normal society and the issues which offer life in the fullest sense. The paradox in all four positions, however, lies in the fact that each disabled person is trying to make a statement which may be valued more for its inspirational value than for the message it purports to convey.

All images of Christ are extremely powerful. Every Christian harbours in their heart a yearning for the Christ they know and understand. The image of Christ, victorious and risen, is the image that the Church finds most acceptable. Within this image it is all too easy to lose contact with the inherent paradox within any discussion of power. The history of Christ's life is one of powerlessness. He hung helpless from the cross and was continually victimised by those in the establishment who offered a comfortable religion to the Jews of the time.

The cross represents the revelation of God's love within the Trinity. The love of God has taken the nature of a man who, in his human frailty, feels both rejected by God and is rejected by men. The love through Christ is exalted on Easter Sunday yet we cannot neglect the rejection of Good Friday. A triumphalistic Christ whose power is all-pervading neglects to show the weakness of Jesus which was God's acceptance of all that is unacceptable in human society. In the cry from the cross, Jesus cried and still cries with the disabled as indeed he does today. This reality must be held together by understanding the triumph of Christ in the light of his sufferings, and by holding the two events so close together that they cannot be accepted into a dogma which holds the triumph as the main facet of Christ's life. I believe that disabled people will have more understanding of Christ if we consider the tension of Easter rather than simply concentrating on the victory. Good Friday is not a step on the way; it is the key. It is now possible for us to present a statement of Christ's involvement with disability.

The appeal of Jesus Christ lies in his acceptance of our lot. He identifies with us; he stands with us, and is continually suffering death for us. Christ shows his identification in his self-giving dealings with people who had all the prejudices of the time against the disabled.

> Jesus was preaching the message to them when four men arrived, carrying a paralysed man to Jesus. Because of the crowd, however, they could not get the man to him. So they made a hole in the roof right above the place where Jesus was. When they had made an opening, they let the man down, lying on his mat. Seeing how much faith they had, Jesus said to the paralysed man, 'My son, your sins are forgiven'. Some teachers of Law who were sitting there thought to themselves, 'How does he dare talk like this? This is blasphemy! God is the only one who can forgive sins!' At once Jesus knew what they were thinking, so he said to them, 'Why do you think such things? Is it easier to say to this paralysed man, "Your sins are forgiven", or to say, "Get up, pick up your mat, and walk"? I will prove to you, then, that the Son of Man has authority on earth to forgive sins'. So he said to the paralysed man, 'I tell you, get up, pick up your mat, and go home!' While they all watched,

the man got up, picked up his mat, and hurried away. They were all completely amazed and praised God, saying, 'We have never seen anything like this!'

(Mark 2:2–12)

The man who came to Jesus came with the dependence of a disabled person. He was carried by his friends. We know not whether he desired to come or not, but when confronted with the man Jesus, he placed his dependence upon him. Turning from the faith of the paralysed man's friends, Jesus entered into dialogue with the man himself. He offered him forgiveness, and this forgiveness was accepted by the man but rejected by all around. He offered him the opportunity to stand and be whole, and this the man did. Whilst many praised God, the teachers of the Law added this to the list of charges which would eventually send Jesus to the cross. The man's suffering had made him dependent upon his friends; Jesus' divine authority offered that man liberation yet dependence on one who would not bind him by the nature of his disability. However, the cost to Jesus was to be borne with him to the cross—the charge of blasphemy made by the scribes who had little understanding of what had happened. This exegesis is largely based on that of Professor Alan E Lewis who sums up the transaction rather dramatically thus:

An incarnation had occurred in which ... the healer had become the cripple, despised and rejected, weakened with the afflictions of others, sick with the diseases, and for them disfigured by an ugliness (as some archetypal Elephant Man?), from which faces turned away.[6]

The full weight of Levitical law had come to rest upon Jesus. He had lifted the burden from the disabled to carry it himself. In so doing he had become the sinner, he accepted rejection and, as the letter to the Hebrews reminds us, he was sent from the city to be crucified outside the wall. As we saw earlier, Jesus continually released people to become free to worship God and be integrated into society; but each time he did so, he reinforced his own isolation and unacceptability.

The theme of isolation is one that is very apparent in the preaching of Peter in the early Acts of the Apostles. In the sermon (Acts 4), following the miracle at Solomon's Porch in which Peter healed a man in the name of Christ, Peter preaches about Christ's rejection by the Jewish authorities and cites verse 22 of Psalm 118:

> 'Jesus is the one of whom the scripture says,
>   "The stone that you the builders despised
>   turned out to be the most important of all".'

(Acts 4:11)

Peter is aware that Jesus was unacceptable in the eyes of the authorities and that he had to be explained to them in terms of the 'Servant Songs'. It does not much matter whether these songs are about Israel, or prophecies about Jesus on which he could model his life, or as texts which were useful to Peter. It matters, rather, that these texts expressed the full weakness of Christ. In his weakness he did not have the power to protest and he went to his suffering in silence (see Isa. 53).

The 'Servant Songs' in Isaiah are very important to our portrayal of the way of the cross. They can be found as distinct prophecies by Isaiah in Isaiah 42:1–4, 49:1–6, 50:4–9, 52:13 and 53:12.

These songs show the paradox of humiliation and proclamation. Israel was humiliated by the Exile, and the once proud race had been stripped of its dignity and left to weep by the rivers of Babylon while their captors laughed. God's people now suffered in a way which was to find a place in the Canon of the Prophecies. Whilst our knowledge of the Holocaust remains outwith the Canon, it has been absorbed into contemporary Jewish liturgy. The Jews of the Exile were stripped of their dignity in the same way as modern victims of car accidents are. Their corporate personalities were abused in the same way in which the personalities of the disabled can be crushed by the incessant prejudice of many uninformed members of society. Yet within such humiliation, it was still possible to proclaim God's word from the depths which Isaiah could see leading to the new Restoration. Isaiah at least could accept the humiliated personalities of the Servant who was going to proclaim yet again Salvation to Israel and to the world.[7] The emaciation was unimportant compared with the hope which lay in the future.

The people reply,
'Who would have believed what we now report?
  Who could have seen the Lord's hand in this?
It was the will of the Lord that his servant
  should grow like a plant taking root in dry ground.
He had no dignity or beauty
  to make us take notice of him.
There was nothing attractive about him,
  nothing that would draw us to him.
We despised him and rejected him;
  he endured suffering and pain.
No one would even look at him —
  we ignored him as if he were nothing.'

(Isa. 53:1–3)

'After a life of suffering, he will again have joy;
  he will know that he did not suffer in vain.
My devoted servant, with whom I am pleased,
  will bear the punishment of many
    and for his sake I will forgive them.
And so I will give him a place of honour,
  a place among great and powerful men.
He willingly gave his life
  and shared the fate of evil men.
He took the place of many sinners
  and prayed that they might be forgiven.'

(Isa. 53:11–12)

If we understand Christ as typifying the vulnerability of God, we begin to identify salvation in a new light. God suffered through his servant Israel as he was later to suffer through the death of his Son Jesus, but because that was so much more personal the suffering was more intense upon the cross. God now understands our suffering and our revulsion at the thought of it. He accepts the anger which is vented upon him by those who lose dear ones or find themselves paraplegic after a very active life; he accepts fully their anger — and in so doing their suffering becomes Christ's suffering and, as a result, it becomes anulled. The triumphant Christ strides over the realm of despair and of suffering, trampling them to the ground, whilst at the same time hanging pathetically from the cross waiting for us to recognise this humiliated figure as the beginning of our salvation. Good Friday and

Easter Sunday are inseparable. It is Christ's nature always to represent both. This our intellect understands, but our psyche can only perceive these events one at a time. Therefore the suffering, or the service, comes before the glory, and continually interacts as we unfold Christ's ministry. The disabled person is now invited to enter into God's mind because he has the privilege of bearing the same stigma which God's Son bore and showing the same endurance which Jesus did to the end. With this knowledge, the disabled person is asked to move forward and accept the offer of life within society where his disability, his stigma, is not counted against him.

This chapter commenced by considering the desire of disabled people to express themselves. Such a drive is shared by those who are Christian and non-Christian alike. The Christian, having recognised Christ's identification, has to make a choice between life and death (See Deut. 30:19). Throughout this book we have seen how several disabled people have found life in Christ and been reassured by the love of God. Fortified with this knowledge of a Christ who is fully identified with the position of the disabled, the disabled person has the ability to forget his affliction and to serve Christ in a new and exciting way. The way of the cross no longer becomes a burden thrust upon him but one which he is willing to accept for the sake of others. The disabled person transcends his disability and may choose a way of the cross which means fighting for the rights of others, or broadening their horizons to take in the suffering of the world in many of its different aspects. The issues which face all Christians today are issues which, to a greater or lesser extent, carry death. Spiritual death comes with the exclusion of the disabled; it comes with the support of nuclear weapons; it is portrayed in the gratuitous violence of television, and it is appeased by us when we offer charity to the starving of the Third World without considering our contribution to their predicament. Many who write creatively are well aware of all these issues and find life in embracing the antidotes to the death which lies within such matters. The disabled person can and does find life in his writing, and in his involvement in escaping from the constraints of a society which would handicap him.

In the second part of this book, we are going to ask why the

Church often fails to accept, and how it could better serve the disabled person. At this stage, however, it seems important to say that the Church appears to fail to attract them to faith. In the broadest sense possible its evangelism fails to have any impression upon the vast majority of the disabled. It may well be that we are concerned in the Church but fail to give acceptable answers and I am offering my own only as a suggestion. Our God is limited by his perfect nature perceived by 'perfect' people. Christ is limited by his triumphalism. The faith that has inspired many is prescriptive in its nature. It is possible to encourage people to understand God's Divine Plan and to accept cheerfully the consequences of this. It is possible in terms of psychology to explain and to understand many disabilities, yet it is impossible to understand God's involvement other than to say as a last resort, 'God's ways are not our ways'. It is possible to be inspired by the courage of the disabled, when in fact it is not courage but resilience or 'sheer guts'.[8] Any homiletic that presents God as one who is a panacea for all ills is bound to fail. Any interpretation of the Bible which is literalistic is often an insult to the intelligence of disabled people, and when we portray Jesus as a good example of how we should bear our suffering, we in fact drag him from the cross and reconstitute him as an unthinking martyr, and thus find ourselves guilty of Docetism. Christ's suffering is not an example to us, it is an illustration of the mind of God. God fully identifies with our predicament and accepts us, not when we are at our strongest, but when we are at our weakest. The moment of anger and of rebellion, the moment when the world becomes black because of failure to hope for acceptance, of gaining the love of the opposite sex, of seeing the passing of caring parents, is the moment when God declares that he stands beside us. He 'descends into hell' with us. The question 'Why?' does not enter into it; but the question 'What has God done?' does.

God stands as the disabled person stands; he in fact offers no answer but gives him the opportunity to grasp a liberation and a new personality which will equip him for life.

It is impossible to describe the blackness with which disabled people can regard the future. It is impossible to relate how suicidal teenagers can become when they see what they are missing from life. It is impossible to describe or indeed to understand what it is like to lie paralysed on a hospital bed, fed, toiletted, washed by strangers who enter the realms of one's existence. It is impossible to recount the dignity which is lost as one grows old, or as arthritis limits one's movements, and deafness or blindness shut out the good world once enjoyed. Yet every day the media portrays the story of someone who has successfully overcome these very problems. In the suffering Christ, disabled people have the chance to find companionship, but in the Christ which is purely prescriptive they lose that which could be very dear to them.

The future is to be feared. There are so many ways of manipulating Christ to an end that it becomes very difficult to find any truth. Any theology which is put forward as being suitable for the disabled person must be done with humility, and with a recognition that many others have found God by a different route. All these routes may be in order and may be correct, but if they do not allow real freedom they are lacking in some way. One question has been begged in this discussion: What is freedom? Freedom is the ability to accept and to be accepted. The truly accepted disabled person is often embarrassed because his friends forget that he is disabled. They cease to make allowances when perhaps they are necessary, and they are not aware of the difficulties which lie in the disabled person's compensation. Christ offers himself to everyone. It is for the Church to make sure that when Christ is received, it is a liberating spirit.

It would be a contradiction to condemn any of the other theologies discussed; they all have their place, they all help. Each has given meaning to someone where life might have been meaningless. But in terms of building an evangelical approach to the many unchurched, uncared for people, the Church must be radical and bold in its presentation, and make absolutely certain that it never constricts Christ by its own unwillingness to admit his weakness, and indeed the potential weakness of every member. We preach often that power comes through weakness. As liberal Christians we adore Gandhi and many other non-violent civil rights leaders. The disabled are going to have to follow the same course, and if the Church is to be in the vanguard, there is no other way;

no prescription will do, only understanding of the mind of God, the one who can bear suffering and stigma, when all other efforts to love mankind have failed.

It is now necessary to look at ways in which the Church can help practically. Theology and stated concern for all disabled people can be lost if the Church cannot also place the practical challenge of accepting disabled people in to their midst, and indeed into their leadership as either laymen or ordained ministers.

Notes to Chapter 4

1 *Newsletter No 2 Spring 1985* (SPUC Handicap Division)
2 Stephen T Davis (editor) *Encountering Evil* (John Knox Press, Atlanta, 1981), p61
3 Dorothee Sölle, *Suffering*, p22 ff
4 Francis MacNutt, *Healing* (Ave Maria Press, Indiana, 1974) p64 ff
5 Kristine Gibbs, *Only One Way Up* (Darton, Longman and Todd, London, 1981)
6 Alan E Lewis, 'God as Cripple: Disability, Personhood and the Reign of God' from *Pacific Theological Review* (Volume XVI, no 1) (San Francisco, 1982)
7 Peter R Ackroyd, *Exile and Restoration* (SCM Press, London, 1968) p127 ff
8 Margaret B Davidson, *You Tell Me* (Scottish Council for Spastics, Edinburgh, 1977)

Part Two

Statement from VI Assembly of the World Council of Churches

Churches are urged to:

1 initiate and pursue study/action programmes leading to preventing disabilities from whatever cause—environmental, nutritional, accidental, or as a result of unjust social, economic and political situations—rehabilitating those in need, using the resources and means available locally;

2 concretely affirm that all persons with disabilities are living stones in the house of God, by including them in the decision-making bodies of the churches at all levels;

3 examine with congregations the factors which hinder the integration and participation of persons with disabilities and take concrete steps to remove them (including the architectural barriers);

4 encourage and facilitate mutual support among families with one or more disabled member, collaborating with existing services where available, and creating such services where necessary;

5 introduce special courses related to persons with disabilities in the theological training programmes;

6 take the initiative to introduce educational programmes in the regular schools to help foster better relations between the children with disabilities and other children;

7 conduct surveys to identify all the people with disabilities in their congregations as a first step towards their integration in the life of the Church (as far as possible this should be an ecumenical effort);

8 offer the sacraments to people with physical and mental disabilities (we are convinced that the disabled people can also have a spiritual understanding of the sacrament and that they are able to participate in their own way in the spiritual life of the Church and the congregation);

9 reconsider how the disabled may have access to ordained ministry;

10 accept persons with disabilities as students and teachers in theological and training schools and colleges.

Official Report, VI Assembly World Council of Churches, Vancouver, Canada 24 July–10 August, 1983.

5

The Church and Integration

A minister, in fact myself, was once looking for a helper for a disabled person who wanted to go swimming in a private pool. I tried the physiotherapy department in the local hospital and from there in despair went to the Social Work department. After a long chat with the social worker it was suggested that I myself had, after all, great influence over the largest voluntary organisation in the town, obligated to 'doing good'. We as Church members tend to regard ourselves not as a voluntary organisation nor as a charity, but wholly as a Church. Yet to the outsider it is very often judged by its meritorious works rather than by any theological definition. This is perhaps one of the reasons why the Salvation Army is universally popular.

In 1984 there were 1 876 840 Church members in Scotland. In that year the Church of Scotland claimed to have a membership of 907 920. The Roman Catholic Church, using slightly different methods of calculation, claimed a membership of 814 400. The report covering all Churches in Scotland claimed that 17 per cent of the Scottish population attended church every Sunday, a figure of 672 760.[1] There is, therefore, within Scotland or any other country a vast number of people who could be tapped to work for the good of disabled people.

Statistics can distort and even give an inaccurate impression especially when they are extrapolated from various surveys. If Churches are fully representative of their community, and find that their fellowship on Sunday at Divine Worship reflects this, there should be within the Churches of Scotland on a Sunday morning 20 182 disabled people. This figure works out at almost three per cent of the population who attend Church on a Sunday.

These figures are purely speculative. It is doubtful whether more disabled people attend Church than is suggested but it is certainly likely to be less. The figures have been extrapolated from those produced by McConkey and McCormack who have suggested figures per 100 000 of the population based on DHSS statistics of some time ago. The following is their list per 100 000 people in the population:

700   people with severe physical impairments
          (Cerebral Palsy, Multiple Sclerosis, Paraplegia)
270   people with visual impairments
300   people with severe hearing impairments
350   mentally handicapped persons (moderate and
          severe)
250   mildly mentally handicapped persons (in receipt of
          special services)

The remaining 1100 or so who are handicapped will have disabilities which do not materially affect their capacity to take care of themselves, but do limit their lifestyle.[2]

Church-going is a very selective activity and we must consider why disabled people might find themselves excluded from Church either because of their own feelings or because they are handicapped by the attitude of Church leaders towards them. The fact remains, however, that the Church is a vast body of people committed to the ministry of Christ, the ministry of compassion, of healing and of wholeness. The disappointed host who could not find guests at his banquet sent his servants out to the highways and the byways (Luke 14:16–24) for the poor and the lame, and according to Christ's parable, they came back with so many that the banquetting hall was filled.[3] It would be very difficult for the Churches of today to accommodate all the poor and lame in their banquetting halls, but have they succeeded in inviting three per cent of their population into their midst? The Church in this country at least does not appear to have the ability to extend Christ's invitation. There may well be two reasons for this: *first*, the disabled may not wish to accept the invitation; and *second*, it is more likely that they cannot. Let us therefore paint fictional profiles of one handicapped person who refuses the invitation, and one who cannot accept much to her disappointment. Robert is an elder of the Church of Scotland. He is married with two grown-up children, one daughter and one son, who both live fairly near to home. He is 63 years of age, very fit except for progressive cataracts. His impaired eye-sight has deprived him of his driving licence and compelled him to take early retirement from his post as a branch manager of a large building society. He is active and goes for long walks with his wife and sometimes the rest of the family. In his life he has contributed a great deal to his church; as an elder he was greatly appreciated for his wisdom and his sense of judgment, and as an ex-Boys' Brigade officer he regarded the Church Company with a fatherly affection. He goes to the church every Sunday with his wife who is terribly aware of his isolation. He no longer does door duty because he cannot recognise people. He is concerned that soon he will have to give up serving at Communion, because the chancel steps are outwith his range of vision. He cannot go to the session at night because he thinks it would be an unfair imposition on his wife, and no one else has offered to take him because he covers up his problem so well. He is exceedingly anxious about the future because his wife may not be able to drive for ever.

Unfortunately, his minister is tempted (however understandable) to see him as yet another 'back-sliding' elder! Ministers often get very despondent when people do not attend to their duties for no apparent reason. The problem with Robert is two-fold; his minister has never thought to counsel him, nor does Robert wish to be counselled. His minister's excellent sermons in church are never addressed to those who might be suffering from a disability and Robert would find it difficult to confess to the minister that he is more than slightly angry with God. He is angry with his fellow elders for not realising that he requires a lift to the session meetings; he is also afraid that the Boys' Brigade will not invite him to their display night this year. What he really needs is the chance to see God in a new light and to understand him as one who identifies with his increasing difficulties and his resentment at being disabled. He would actually be very surprised if his minister attempted to offer him a new vision of God; his faith has been stoically received and understood throughout his life, and now it would be wrong to bring to his notice a new image of Christ. He is shocked enough by the pronouncements of certain leading Churchmen, let alone his own minister. It would appear, therefore, that he is condemned to a new kind of rejection of God; a lapsing for no good reason and a growing unease with his status compared with his state of belief. But Robert's problem is not one of belief. He does not require to encounter Christ for the first time, but rather to begin to see Christ in a dynamic way being aware of Christ's involvement in human situations. It takes courage to realise that the triumphalism of Christ is perhaps a barrier to faith. The minister must try to develop a new theology for Robert's predicament and to counsel him accordingly. If he does not, Robert will lapse into bitterness, and in a very short time retreat. He will then lose a vast part of the meaning of his previous life psychologically as well as physically.

Janice is 21 years old, suffers from cerebral palsy, spends her life in a wheelchair and does not ever expect to walk. Her dexterity is good and likewise her speech, although many are deceived by her involuntary movements caused by athetosis. Janice has enjoyed a good secondary education and has been given the opportunity to take a vocational course in secretarial skills. She has travelled widely with groups organised by her special school and whilst at further education college. She reads a great deal and on one of her trips she encountered an evangelical group who introduced her to what is now a very strong faith. She has been unable to buy a car even with the benefit of generous hire-purchase terms and she has not gained employment. On the few occasions when she has omitted to state that she is disabled on her application, she has received a polite but disinterested interview. The churches closest to her are all pseudo-Gothic in design and quite unsuitable for wheelchairs. The pews are fixed and there are flights of stairs at the entrances followed by awkward doors in the church. She was very sad when she recently felt she had to turn down a wedding invitation from one of her best friends. She was conscious that the sight of so many people carrying her into church would have detracted from the splendour of the occasion.

Janice manages to live on her own in a house adapted by the Council but is stuck in the corner of the estate almost as if she is to be segregated along with the old-age pensioners. She manages to live on her severe disablement allowance of £23.25 per week. She also receives mobility allowance which she tries to save for the eventual purchase of a car, but which she often uses to boost her standard of living. Between her mobility allowance and the generosity of her family she manages to buy some luxuries which otherwise would be denied to her. Her mobility allowance is often frittered away on quite unnecessary taxi journeys to the DHSS office and other places. Because of the financial constraints on her lifestyle she cannot get out much and does not travel a great deal. She is very isolated from the rest of the community and would love to be involved in the activities of the young people in the church which is totally beyond her. It would help her greatly if there was publicity about the church, if she knew who to contact about transport, for example, or about use of her talents. Her longing to be valued by church people is one which could easily be fulfilled, but has so far eluded all the power of the over-churched town in which she lives.

These two profiles have been concocted so that we may draw out some of the important matters with which the Church at large and individual churches must grapple if they are to accept disabled people in the community into their midst. We shall assume that the theology has been taken care of and move to some practical matters which are listed below.

Isolation: Disabled people are very isolated and find that their main source of entertainment comes from either self-made activities, the television, or close family.

Communication: There is insufficient communication between disabled people and those who control institutions in society, including the Church.

Access: If congregations are going to be welcoming fellowships it is necessary that the buildings are also welcoming. Furthermore, it is important that as a body of Christians they use their influence to think about changes in the overall physical environment.

Employment: Christians have a responsibility to take employment of disabled people seriously.

Benefits: These should be re-distributed more to help the poor in our midst.

Religion: Religious activities should be all-inclusive, and churches should take to heart the recommendations of the World Council of Churches.[4]

Isolation

Congregations include a number of organisations concerned with education. Education begins with the child in Sunday School and continues with the adult, although the adult is generally channelled into Bible Study groups or the Woman's Guild, whilst adolescents may become involved in a Youth Fellowship. These organisations may be used to combat isolation. The problem cannot be overcome merely by organising lifts, by removing insuperable barriers, or simply by preaching a theology which is acceptable to disabled people. Isolation is basically caused because of the barriers of ignorance. Disabled people who may be invited by well-intentioned groups to join in their functions may be acutely embarrassed by the awkwardness with which they are received, and the event to which they are invited may in fact reinforce their isolation. Organisations within the Church must combat attitudes which would isolate disabled people by engaging in community education. We have already hinted at how many disabled are within one given parish; how can organisations reach out to understand their problems?

They must make the effort to use suitable material to educate themselves. There is not a great deal of evidence of Sunday School material which actually incorporates images of disabled people. There is no need to single them out for Sunday School attention, but stories can be thus re-written that a spastic or a Down's syndrome child can be included quite naturally. If it can be organised in this way for soap operas, it can be organised for Sunday School material. School children can be asked to imagine the miracles from the point of view of the person being healed, rather than from a viewpoint which simply shows the glory of Jesus. Sunday School can examine the problems of access within the members' own church. Children can be asked to manoeuvre around the church in a wheelchair or to feel their own way round as blind members of the community. We must not forget that many of them are watching grandparents growing older and having to deal with certain disabilities; we can help them to enter into an imaginative appreciation of the grandparents' predicaments.

Youth Fellowships and Guilds use videos and invite speakers to talk on the problems of disability, but they must be aware that the purpose of any such meeting can be lost unless they plan to have a follow-up. They should assure themselves that at least one stated aim can come out of any meeting, and the chairman or president ought to be prepared to make this point. In the small group people can resolve to undertake little things that may be important to them. It is insufficient to be moved by a film or by a speaker, yet be unprepared to consider the situation which they, the audience, the spectators, have created. If there is a collection would it not be better to spend the money on their own church or organisation than on a major charity? If a disabled person presents a cause on behalf of, say, a pro-life organisation, should some of the audience not consider joining in, using their own time, or could they not consider inviting the same speaker back, so that as a group they might become willing to integrate fully with a certain group of handicapped people whom they understand after a long dialogue? The presentation must be entertaining, but only in the sense that it holds the group's attention; the after effect is what is important. The book *Breaking the Barriers* deals with all kinds of community education and is well worth consulting in this context; as one would realise, this book is about programmes of education and it must be stressed that one-off talks are not going to solve the diverse problems which are before us.

There is another exercise which could be undertaken. Several years ago the Board of Social Responsibility of the Church of Scotland sent a questionnaire to all ministers in order to elicit how much they knew or did not know about alcoholism. It was their intention to publish a report based on this questionnaire and to supply an information pack; this has been greatly appreciated by many ministers. A similar questionnaire could be produced about the disabled. The difficulty is that very few of us are willing to acknowledge that we are ignorant and would resent having to answer questions on so many issues related to disability. The outcome, however, might be that an information pack could be produced for ministers and office-bearers. In the meantime ministers cannot be urged often enough to buy the *Directory for Disabled People* and to consult it regularly. Again, in every kind of group, questionnaires can also form the foundation for a discussion group. By encouraging people to commit their opinions to paper, they feel that they have contributed to the evening, and they can then compare notes and discover the strengths and weaknesses of other members in the group.

Communication

Communication becomes a priority in the programme of integrating disabled people into the life of the Church. They have a message which is new and exciting to share with the Church at large. Their isolation may be broken by the willingness of congregations to listen, to share and possibly to receive the satisfaction of a positive and mature feedback. However, some Churches are inhospitable and the function of the Courts in the Presbyterian tradition is such that they are not amenable to those in wheelchairs or to those who cannot be active in the running and upkeep of the church. Because they cannot find a way to carry out their functions from wheelchairs, with blindness, or most often with deafness, there tends to be no place for the disabled person in the Kirk Session and likewise in the other courts of the Church. The challenge before them to speak is an enormous one to which I will return later. Kristine Gibbs found that it was exceedingly difficult to speak in her professional social work body. The physical and mental strain in the excitement of doing so almost ruined the marvellous contribution she had to make. Her insight is so valuable that it is worth quoting in this chapter, and at a later stage her inward feelings as she approached the rostrum of the social work conference.

'The inevitable was becoming terrifyingly plain. I would have to speak in case nobody else did. Still I hesitated. Would they listen? Would the trauma of having to speak in a room full of people make my disability worse, perhaps reducing me to silence? Would I make a fool of myself? I realised that this would be relatively unimportant; if I did not speak and the amendment was passed unchallenged, the guilt from my cowardice would live with me for a long time.'[5]

The end which disabled people wish to achieve is that of influencing their peer-groups in ways which are appropriate and normal to any person. The Church is challenged more and more to give them access to influence. We must think in terms of 'positive discrimination' as indeed we have with women; and we must be aware that we are going to be presented with new insights based upon the novelty of such participation for the first time. These voices will be sometimes wrong, sometimes strident, often unacceptably challenging, but nevertheless the authentic voice of a minority within the Church. If these voices are heard, we will have begun to integrate as we never thought possible.

The Church has already integrated one group of disabled people very successfully. These are the deaf and dumb congregations. They play their parts in the courts of the Church; they can present some beautiful arts in the form of deaf and dumb choirs visibly acceptable to many; and they show that congregations can be run by those who are disabled. The case I am pleading is that we should extend the power to people with other disabilities and wherever possible do so within the context of an able-bodied congregation.

Access
St Columba's Church, which is one of the churches within the congregation of Hoy and Walls (Orkney), was recently renovated at a cost of over £70 000. In keeping with the sentiments of this book, a ramp was constructed up to one of the doors, and the doors themselves were made wide enough for wheelchairs. The advantage of this highly commendable item of expenditure was short lived because a thick gravel path was laid from the road up to the ramp and the disabled person whom we thought might attend church was once again excluded because his wheelchair could not cope with the gravel. This shows us that in practice access is a very technical subject. Our desire to obey the letter of the law, or indeed the spirit of the law can so easily be undermined by our lack of knowledge

of the problems. Gravel was simply forgotten about, just as hotels tend to forget about the impracticality of spring doors, long piled carpets, and suitable entrances to bedrooms, when they are planning otherwise perfectly designed buildings. When volunteers have gone for training in the skills of surveying access, many have felt the benefit of exploring the building in a wheelchair rather than simply being shown round.

The problem with our churches is that many were designed for the fit Victorian worshipper. Modern day congregations must have the motivation to adapt buildings, planners the insight to change, and architects the technical knowledge to execute these changes. Congregations have to exercise common sense. Very often now a condition of a grant is that a toilet will be provided. This toilet must certainly comply with all the codes of practice related to its accessibility, and further-more, if the congregation is to economise to meet these standards, they should do so by making the toilets unisex. Access ramps should be built wherever possible, pews moved to accommodate wheelchairs, and suitable seats supplied to accommodate arthritic people. If at all possible, the chancel should be completely accessible to wheelchairs and any reno-vation to a pulpit should include the same requirements. Eyemouth Parish Church is a very good example of how this can be achieved in a building which is not very conducive to radical alteration.

A congregation needs the will-power to carry out renovations which incorporate access for the disabled. The renovations will be costly and probably, as the congregation ages, the necessity will become more acute. The renovations will have to be co-ordinated whereas quite often they are piecemeal. For instance, many public buildings have very good disabled toilets. The will has been there to make a gesture, but the route to the toilet may have doors that are unsuitable, and bends in the corridors, and small insignificant steps that have been left untouched. The tokenism of the toilet becomes totally irrelevant. Congregations ought to counter this ten-dency by having a disabled person on the planning committee. If such a person is not available within the congregation (which we have seen is unlikely), one should be recruited from a neighbouring congregation. This would be in accord with the Chronically Sick and Disabled Persons Act of 1981 and of the attitude of the Scottish local authorities who have led the field in appointing liaison officers to deal with access.

Architects and chartered surveyors ought to be fully aware of all Codes of Practice and British Standards.[6] Some of the Standards are mentioned in legislation, and an appropriate place to begin to learn them is in Goldsmith's book *Designing for the Disabled*.[7] Architects ought to include adaptations for the disabled, and they should feel unable to undertake work which does not include considerable research and effort into finding ways to accommodate their needs. Planners and grant-assisting bodies are other groups who can influence access. Many church buildings are either completely free from planning regulations or are tied to the condition of grants. Wherever possible, churches should conform to the standards laid down for other public buildings in the community, and they should also be aware of the power which planning and safety officers have in restricting access for the disabled or in encouraging it. When I spoke earlier of Britain as a 'neurotic society', I was referring to Peter Large's comments on fire regulations which may be necessary, but which become excessive when they ban wheelchairs in places of entertainment and may restrict employment in certain occupations. There is evidence that church halls will have to comply more and more with such regulations, but congregations and architects alike must make sure that every provision is made to ensure that disabled people are not restricted by over-fussy considerations of public safety.

The sum and substance of access is that facilities for the disabled which are visibly available, act as signs of the willingness of churches to integrate the handicapped and make them welcome. Private discussions, public and private debates and doctrine, and congregational generosity to charities benefiting people with disabilities, all can be undermined if the signs of goodwill are not present.

Employment
The Church as an institution is not a large employer, but a significant one. There is not a great deal of scope for employ-

ment at the local level but when we consider the bureaucracy of the Church and the wide ranging obligations to the social services which it undertakes, the number of employees rises quite significantly. The employment of disabled ministers will be raised in chapter seven, but here we must consider other forms of employment. Do we as a Church spend sufficient time thinking of how many clerical posts can be filled by disabled people, who are adequately trained but confined to a wheelchair? The headquarters of the Church of Scotland is not even readily accessible by wheelchair, nor can its staff accept that with increasing computerisation a great deal of employment could be offered to a disabled clerk or clerkess. Similarly do we employ sufficient disabled people in our Eventide Homes, and other social work agencies? Generous grants are made available by the Manpower Services Commission to adapt premises for the employment of the disabled, and similar monies could be made available for church premises. Successive reports by the Church and Nation Committee of the General Assembly of the Church of Scotland have stressed that work should not be measured by whether it is paid employment, or by its status, but by its social usefulness. If congregations adapt their premises, ministers could adapt their working schedules and disabled people could be offered socially satisfying work.

In a wider sphere the Church can take an active interest in promoting other industrial ventures for the disabled. One such venture was investigated at length by Strathclyde University in a feasibility study financed by the Jubilee Trust and instigated by a group of Christians. A group of Christians in Livingston envisaged the possibility of setting up a workshop to adapt cars for the disabled, employing disabled people both skilled and unskilled, and also using those with professional qualifications. Unfortunately the feasibility study proved that this would not be viable and nothing came of the scheme. Nevertheless, the sentiments and purpose behind it of employing able and bright disabled people in a creative and inventive manner are indicative of the sorts of projects that ought to be pursued by church members more vigorously. Employers should exhibit their Christian convictions in their workplace by accepting, willingly at least, the three per cent

quota laid down by law. They should make a point of employing more disabled. Finally, they should exploit all government grants to enable them to adapt their premises for the
disabled.

Benefits
A congregation may seek to integrate disabled people into its
fellowship, and with good will on all sides it may well succeed.
Members of the congregation may feel moved to join groups
which support disabled people but they must realise that
when it comes to caring there must be a reckoning in terms of
cost. There are two kinds of cost: that of providing care and
welfare for the disabled; and the cost of love, or charity as the
Authorised Version of the Bible calls it, which is a spiritual
cost.

Benefits to and for the disabled come in four distinct forms.
First, the benefits of the health service. This may well become
a topic of another book in the series, but we must observe that
many handbooks for the disabled published in America have
chapters on health and finance and family insurance. We in
this country should be very proud and relieved that our
disabled are cared for freely and according to need. Financial
provision for the care of the disabled has increased greatly
over the years and has done so in steps. The polio epidemics
of the nineteen-thirties increased the provision of care, as did
the thalidomide catastrophe. Each time a need has been met it
has resulted in new clinics, more sophisticated technology and
new specialisms.

Second, unlike the health service and social security benefits,
many of the local benefits are paid out of rates. Local authorities in the past have paid fees to special schools, and social
work departments have been obliged by various Acts, to act
on behalf of disabled people. In the field of education, there
has been a move away from special schools run specifically for
a particular disability and much more emphasis has been
placed upon regional schools for a multiplicity of disabilities.
Since the report of the Warnock Committee in 1978, ordinary
schools have been obliged to make every effort to integrate the
disabled into their own timetable, curriculum and environment.

The Social Work department of every local authority has

obligations placed upon it. They have discretionary powers to offer grants to charities such as the Disablement Income Group (DIG), and to provide telephones, home helps and holidays to relieve the strenuous efforts of many caring relatives. These powers are mainly discretionary and lamentably under used; so much so that the groups which they support, such as DIG become rods with which to beat their own backs. These groups continually point out to local authorities how they are failing to meet these needs, and sometimes they fortunately succeed in increasing provisions. But Social Work departments are over-stretched by the community care for the psychiatrically ill and the mentally handicapped. There are simply not enough funds or resources available from our rates to meet all the needs of local provisions.

Third, disabled people benefit greatly from allowances from the Department of Health and Social Security. These benefits are met from our taxes and are characterised by their complexity, their arbitrariness and inflexibility. Disabled people benefit from many different payments, but basically have to qualify by being eligible for one or more of the few deliberately targeted at them. These benefits include Attendance Allowance, Invalid Care Allowance, Mobility Allowance and Severe Disablement Allowance. On receipt of one of these, one becomes eligible for free prescriptions and health care.[8] Concern has been expressed about the bureaucracy of the DHSS and the need for persistence in achieving all to which one is entitled. The appeal procedures, the means test and the strict medical examinations make all these benefits difficult to obtain and there is now a need for rationalisation. The benefits, which already cost the taxpayer dearly, need to become more comprehensive and more generous. But this means that taxpayers must be willing to shoulder an even greater burden to display their awareness and understanding of the nature of disability.

In the early part of 1987 the Disablement Income Group introduced their latest policy statement on 'National Disablement Income'. In this document they describe a two-stage solution to the problems of the hardships suffered by disabled people and a rationalisation of our present benefit system.[9] The document argues that disabled people can find the cost of living much higher in two ways. All of them have to forgo bargains when they cannot shop around, even although they have enormous replacement costs on clothing items such as shoes, and they have to spend much money on home improvements as necessities not luxuries. It is often the case that the disabled person cannot earn at all and therefore has no scope in which to contribute to the finances of family life or to the necessities of his daily living. The document suggests that disablement be assessed in the same way as industrial injuries, and that awards be made to an extended group of disabled people including children and to those who become disabled in retirement. DIG therefore recommends that an allowance should 'meet the expenses and other difficulties of daily living'; and, also that there should be an 'alternative to earning'. Those who become eligible either as disabled people or parents would receive a disablement costs allowance which might in very severe cases possibly reach £140 a week, but more typically would probably offer benefits of about £25 a week (DIG's figures). Disability would be assessed and the award made accordingly. This would remove many hardships from parents and the disabled alike and would allow the disabled person the choice of how to spend his pension. Such an allowance would be dependent upon the commitment to assessment and to the categorisation of disability, and DIG makes it quite clear that they would not wish to see a flat rate introduced since this would probably favour the less severely disabled to the detriment of others. DIG goes on to argue that it is now necessary to introduce a system of invalidity benefits for those who cannot earn and require care. This benefit should be high enough to meet the normal cost of living and should represent a respectable proportion of the national average wage unlike present allowances. The costs would require considerable social accounting and much work still has to be undertaken to evaluate them. The net result would be to give much greater dignity to the disabled and to create a sense of equality between the disabled and the non-disabled.

Fourth, there are the victims of road accidents, medical mishaps and sporting injuries. The level of compensation should be standardised and should reflect the needs of those who have been paralysed, brain damaged, or otherwise deprived of their previous quality of life. The law and the insurance companies should recognise the merit of 'No Fault' compensation and be prepared to meet all claims at a level which will at least equal the non-contributary pension. Countries such as Canada or New Zealand have proven that 'No Fault', or 'No Blame', systems can be attempted.

Religion

This last section is more general. In the normal course of religious observance of any of its forms of Worship or Rites, the Church does not automatically exclude disabled people. They are excluded because of extraneous circumstances which have already been discussed. However, we must take seriously the call of Christ, and the interpretation of that call through his Apostle Paul, to affirm the New Creation in the body of Christ. The body has many parts and many functions, and disabled people may well have their contribution to make. But it is highly likely that their contribution will only have a spurious connection with their disability. They are however part of the community and therefore part of the secular world which has to be invited into fellowship in the love of God. This means that they must be met and welcomed into the Church as people who are going to rise to their full potential.

It is well known that discrimination and handicapping occurs in open society. This therefore makes it vitally important that the Church stands as a signal of acceptance and normality. Disabled people can be asked to do the most difficult of tasks within the Church and others can learn patience and tolerance to allow them to do so. Of course, in the case of the Ministry this is most obviously apparent, but within the context of the congregation it is equally vital. Disabled people eventually must be invited to represent the Church at every available level. We must not be intimidated by the prejudice of others, but promote disabled people to positions so that they can speak to congregations, administer their affairs, and make decisive policy decisions. This will involve a great deal of learning on the part of congregational members. They will be required to learn how gently to guide blind people around buildings, handle wheelchairs, and how to present their voices in such a way that deaf people can hear them without being shouted at. A great deal of sensitivity will be required among members, and an awareness of the individual needs of people who vary in the form of their disability to a degree which has not yet been realised by the able-bodied. Basic tasks undertaken by office-bearers will have to be altered and adapted for disabled people. There is no reason, for instance, why a disabled person cannot greet members at the door of the Church on Sunday mornings, provided that we understand that he may require the assistance of another office-bearer, and have an awareness of the pitfalls into which we can fall in terms of condescension. We will be asked to consider distributing Communion in new ways. We will require vessels which are easily carried and have more people participating in order that wheelchairs can be pushed.

'The caring congregation', as Wilke points out, achieves such little things more successfully.[10] This will be the congregation which has no fear of disabled people and has adapted its buildings and its general attitudes in order to make life as normal as possible.

The building of the New Creation is a constant struggle by the Church to present Christ's Ministry to the world. The integration of disabled people was part of his ministry and we must look for signs of his Churches' involvement in this process. The signs can be those of a welcoming congregation or a fresh approach to theology. But, now and again, a true sign of total involvement within the community may be achieved. We shall now examine one such sign which was not totally successful, yet points a way forward.

A signal project

I have served in three parishes and in two of them I have felt constrained to do something for disabled people. In Drumchapel, an association for the parents of severely disabled children was set up and they used the church hall or school hall for meetings. At one meeting we sat on the floor propped up by wall bars in the school gym discussing policy. The parents began to express the frustrations of living 24 hours a day with Down's syndrome children and began to appreciate the care and concern of the special schools which were in the area. As an enabler, I was involved only for about six months, but I was pleasantly surprised to discover the association still existed several years later. Parents are very strongly motivated to end the isolation of their children and to have the opportunity of talking about worries and frustrations among understanding people with similar problems.

In Berwick, the situation was a much more promising one in that the congregation could have become greatly involved in the care of disabled people. Unfortunately, their concern remained marginal, but perhaps a more adept minister could have drawn a lot more practical support. The point of contact between congregation and organisation was in the use of church premises and, to a lesser extent, finance. Hopefully by describing this project the reader will see a way forward to tackle some of the problems of the last few pages in a congregational setting.

In 1981, the International Year of the Disabled Person, I and my wife Angela (along with a victim of multiple sclerosis, Dorothy, who has since died) were instrumental in forming an organisation called BAD (Berwick Association for the Disabled). Its aim was to publicise the IYDP and its chosen means were Brains Trusts, Library exhibitions, and, perhaps the most significant, wheelchair dancing by the Westerlea team of spastic children. The most moving sight was to see eightsome reels being performed on a cold, blustery summer day by boys in their kilts and girls in their white crimplene dresses, below the steps of the Town Hall which had for centuries overlooked the busy market of that town. (It is a sign of the latter half of the eighties that due to financial constraints and educational policy such good ambassadors are no longer so readily available.) Angela organised the window displays and the churches were well represented at Brains Trusts which featured the local MP, RADAR field officers and Sue and Kenny Smith. (The Smiths' life in Durham has been remarkable, I might add, not least in the way they have been supported by their local congregation who formed a team to visit the couple morning and night; this made it possible for Kenny to live at home despite his very severe disabilities which necessitated help in dressing and undressing, and so on.)

A few months later BAD was looking for a new *raison d'etre*. It was glibly suggested that a community programme might be sponsored by the group and that they might become the independent sponsors of this project financed by the Manpower Services Commission. Almost overnight the author became manager of a scheme with a budget of £26 000 per annum guaranteed by the MSC. The sheer difficulties of actually being successful in that rôle could occupy many pages itself. Suffice to say that our business acumen gave our financial advisers more than one headache. However, lest we digress too far, let us return to the Church's connection with this venture, which we renamed or reconstructed as the Berwick Council for the Disabled so that we could have the support, guidance and help of the Newcastle Council for the Disabled and RADAR.

The scheme exployed six workers who were either part time or full time. The wages were paid to the Council by the MSC and the yearly budget for running costs was paid mainly by the subsidy of £440 per worker, plus donations from churches and other bodies. £23 000 in the second year went on wages paid by the MSC to the Berwick Council for the Disabled who set wage rates and conditions of employment and hours. The connection with Wallace Green Church was that we turned first one room and then another into accommodation for offices. It was a stroke of genius to strip an unused ladies cloakroom of coat hooks and to bolt an adjoining door to the woman's toilet in order to make an office. A telephone was supplied and planning permission sought for the change in use of premises. The congregation now had in the heart of its premises the potential (a) to fulfil the General Assembly's exhortations to create employment; (b) to learn about disabled people; and (c) to provide a means of answering all the vexing questions of this chapter. The opportunity was not taken up fully, however, and the Council now resides in secular premises rather more promising than those humble beginnings in a converted ladies cloakroom. It is now employing many more disabled people and meeting the needs which were perceived in the early years but which have taken some years to fully develop. (It is impossible to resist the temptation to draw an analogy between a woman's cloakroom and a very famous stable, both of which were used because nothing else was available at the time!)

When the office was established there were five workers plus a manager and the tasks they were set reflected most of the interest of this book. The manager was obviously expected to deal with wages and staff matters but he also was asked to organise further exhibitions. These exhibitions gave the people of Berwick an opportunity to see what adaptations could be made for disabled people and how their lives could be ameliorated by the concern of all the utility industries and by many established charities, such as the British Legion, the Woman's Royal Voluntary Service (WRVS) and the Red Cross. School children were brought to the first exhibition; but subsequent events were more difficult to organise because British Gas and other major firms could not afford to keep returning. However, Angela conceived the idea of a Charities Fair. This was a two-day event in which all the charities working for the disabled in the area were invited, not to compete, but to stand together displaying all their efforts under the same 'umbrella' of the Berwick Council for the Disabled. These Fairs continue to this day but they are now rather too broadly based to be considered purely for and about disabled people. The example of this venture in Berwick could be adopted by many churches and, if properly organised, could promote a great exchange of information and service.

Access is a major concern of local councils for disabled people. The Council in Berwick set about tackling the problem in two ways. The manager received all planning applications and on several occasions, when necessary, objected to the plans of public buildings and attempted to quote appropriate Codes of Practice. We also employed a full time access officer and an assistant who were trained in Newcastle; they proceeded to measure and survey every public building in Berwick. A guide book project took several years to produce and the writer—myself—failed to procure the last copy on a later visit from Orkney, during the first half of 1986.

The other two workers tackled the problem of isolation. The first was a telephonist/typist/receptionist who answered queries either by telephone or by letter. However, Berwick is a very reticent town; it is to be hoped that this service will become more popular as the years pass. The other worker visited homes and simply befriended people, did their shopping and met personal crises.

Since the Council moved to its new premises it has acquired a mini-bus and can offer activities such as swimming for the disabled.

It has to be stated that throughout the early years of involvement with this project, its full potential was not met. This report of its activities describes more of the potentials than the frustrations of the first two years; and a vision of what the church could instigate and be involved in, rather than the end which one would like to see.

Whether it is in Drumchapel, Berwick or perhaps some day in Orkney, it is clear that the disabled people must do something to help themselves. They must cause a revolution which may result in dancing in the streets, and it is for the Church to meet the frustrations and difficulties of an under-privileged minority as it has done throughout the ages. It must undergird its concern, moreover, with a truly Christian service and theology, which is both a sufficient apologia and a practical guide to the problems which will be discussed in the next chapter.

Notes to Chapter 5

1   Peter Brierly (*et al*) *Prospects for Scotland* (National Bible Society of Scotland, Edinburgh, 1985)
2   Roy McConkey and Bob McCormack, *Breaking Barriers*, p 24
3   Harold H Wilke, *Creating the Caring Congregation*, ch 2
4   Roy McConkey and Bob McCormack, *op cit*. Here I am using their methodology.
5   Kristine Gibbs, *Only One Way Up*, p 143 ff
6   *Code of Practice for Access for the Disabled to Buildings* (BS 5810) (British Standards Institution, London, 1979)
7   Selwyn Goldsmith, *Designing for the Disabled* (RIBA Publication, London, 1976)
8   *Help for Handicapped People in Scotland* (Scottish Office, DHSS and Employment Service Agency, Edinburgh, 1976)
9   *DIG's National Disability Income* (Policy Statement, 1987)
10 Harold H Wilke, *Creating the Caring Congregation*, ch 5

6

Love Versus Law:
Some Moral Issues

Christians live in a constant state of tension between the knowledge of the law of God, and the love of God revealed in the Lord Jesus Christ. The reader of Paul's epistles is made aware of the necessity to have the law to control our baser instincts, whereas the love of Jesus Christ elevates us above such instincts, and introduces us to the means of grace and the gifts of the Spirit. We see in Christ how people are brought back to wholeness, whether of body or mind or of spirituality. Christ did not abolish the law, but he has certainly interpreted it in a pure way which involves the development of a heart which is full of love and grace.

Anyone trying to approach the subject of disabled people must become aware of this tension. There are three areas which concern us. *First*, all of us are challenged to consider the wholeness of disabled people. *Second*, we are challenged by the statutes of this land to put aside law and overcome our prejudices against them by love. *Third*, there has been a rapid increase in the 'consumerisation of disability', and this has led to greater opportunities to exploit the disabled for fast profit and to make a rich killing financially.

For many years disabled people have felt that they have been denied their personhood. There is a very real sense in which this has been exaggerated, yet the complaint must be taken seriously. It is felt most acutely by disabled people who have unfortunate labels put upon them. Many terms for the disabled have become terms of abuse—'spastic', 'cretin', or even 'mongol' (which has racial overtones). They have also felt that they have not been allowed to develop their own personalities within their own disabilities. We talk of the 'disabled' rather than groups; our perception is narrowed to those in wheelchairs, when there is a great need to remember those who can walk but are weak in gait, dexterity or one of the five senses. By categorising the disabled we have made certain people more acceptable than others. War wounded are not 'disabled'; nor are the elderly seen as 'disabled' because their disabilities are taken as part of the natural process of ageing. Our openness towards disability must become such that we can indeed strip away the categorisation and recognise the desires of disabled people. Most realise that their condition cannot be cured, and to a certain extent cannot be overcome. It becomes important therefore that we use the correct terms.

As long ago as 1967, I found in America a general campaign to refer to spastics as cerebral palsied people, or people with CP. This campaign has now spread to this country although it has not reached the charities concerned. We do find already in print, references to spina bifida people and to Down's syndrome people. In a sense this trend has increased an awareness of our responsibilities to these groups, whilst at the same time it has perhaps 'sanitised' our understanding and general description of disability. It is a campaign that eventually may bear fruits.

It may legitimately be asked how important all this is to the individual disabled person. I remember being at a Youth Fellowship one night and being addressed by a speaker from a major aid charity. At one point in the talk we were discussing possible activities for fund raising and the suggestion of singing was made. The speaker replied, 'Personally, I'm spastic when I try to sing'. This type of remark immediately diminishes any cerebral palsied person who is present at such a talk. It is important when we open our eyes to the richness and variety of disability that we also see the gifts which God can allow to develop in different ways within disabilities.

We must also escape from the stigma of disability and be prepared to become blind to the outer signs which we so readily categorise. The extent of one's disability becomes part of one's body image and to a certain extent one's attempt to overcome the stigma with one's body-language.[1] When disabled people are rejected for employment or rejected socially, the very nature of their image is being taken to pieces. On many occasions rejection is accompanied by the comment, 'There is nothing personal involved'. Such a comment is cruel and misguided in the extreme. The personhood of the applicant for the job has been attacked most savagely by the unintentional lie on the part of those who have power to influence the course of the disabled person's life.

The next issue in this chapter involves the way British society has sought thus far to accommodate the handicapped in employment, entertainment and education. Successive governments in Britain have sought to achieve the integration of disabled people through voluntary means. They have drawn up statutes and trusted that without heavy-handed enforcement people would obey them. The Chronically Sick and Disabled Persons Act is full of loopholes, and the quota system for employment of disabled people in firms with more than 20 employees can be abused by the very definition of disability. For someone who really wants to thwart the good intention of British regulations, it is very easy to do so. Even at the heart of government, in the Civil Service, much pressure has had to be applied to make the service conform with general principles regarding employment.[2]

When we think of entertainment we consider mainly theatres, cinemas and shopping/leisure centres. The regulations concerning safety are very strict in such establishments and the temptation to ignore the disabled is very great. A slow walker or a wheelchair would be bound to impede the safe and effective evacuation of a building. We have to ask ourselves how the proprietors of such buildings could provide safe access and choice to disabled people in wheelchairs, to the blind and even facilities for the deaf. Avoiding access and accommodation for disabled people is too easily achieved by finding the loopholes in legislation and denying that one can meet the expenditure. In the realms of transport one is acutely aware that speed and safety again should be given more consideration for disabled people. There is also the impression that many staff in public institutions remain untrained and do not see dealing with the disabled as part of their daily work.[3]

Legislation to cover all of these areas has been in existence for many years. It can be argued by disabled people that the legislation has not worked, and equally forceably it can be argued that re-appraisal has now become necessary. The Report by the Committee on Restrictions Against Disabled People (CORAD) illustrates the frustrations and the inner conflicts which disabled people have towards legislation. Once again we have a conflict between love and law. We are faced with the choice of expecting people to improve in their attitudes or falling victim to laws which enforce their compliance. The CORAD report recommends that a Commission be set up to oversee all acts discriminating against disabled people.[4] It would seek to do away with many of the frustrations which the disabled people face. The scope of the proposals has been described in an earlier chapter.

The question remains, however, whether anti-discriminatory legislation would be desirable. Have we now reached such a stage in our caring for disabled people that Christian and non-Christians alike can exercise no more love and will have to be compelled by law to cease discrimination? If there were to be anti-discriminatory laws, disabled people would have to be categorised and it would have to be clear in everyone's mind exactly what constituted disability, which facets of disability allowed exemptions from discrimination, and precisely which areas were to be covered. This would require much research on many different levels and would probably result both in greater awareness of disability and in a compulsion to categorise as never before. For instance, one of the policies recommended is that all disabled people should be allowed access to Life Assurance, subject only to actuarial advice. Whilst it would be good to understand the nature of disabilities, the amount of paper and calculations that would be required to make certain that every disability was treated fairly would give much greater emphasis to the nature of disability. On the other hand, there are those who feel that too much legislation would weaken goodwill and remove love from the situation.[5]

I would argue that the Gospel is such that we must not depend upon the law, but seek to do everything in our power by love. It is our sin and our blindness which keep us from seeing ways of helping to integrate disabled people; it is our discomfiture when we do let them enter into life which fires our need to discriminate against them. If civil law did demand of us that we dropped our prejudice, we might still find that we could victimise in new and more suitable ways.

It seems to me that each disabled person has to journey through life seeking to integrate and be integrated by education and by example. There are many frustrations which could be dealt with by legislation, but with good fortune and perseverance most of these can be overcome voluntarily. The case for legislation remains unproven and we must rather continue to rely upon the individual's ability and skill in dealing with people. The Church of Scotland must be congratulated on its conformity with the plans and schemes contained within the CORAD report. As an employer, the Church of Scotland is fair and honest and could prove to be an example to many others. (However, there are some difficulties and these will be dealt with in the next chapter.)

Another issue: disabled people have always required aids. Children require special chairs, the elderly require lifts, walking aids, grips, and so on; young adults require cars, aids to allow them to work and adapted houses to enable them to live independently. The needs have not changed much in the last 30 years, but circumstances and expectations have. This trend has been called the 'consumerisation of disability'. Thirty years ago special schools, hospitals and government departments employed craftsmen who produced devices, furniture and aids which were very much the result of their ingenuity, skill and dedication to their patients. At Westerlea the carpenter was a very valued member of staff who worked with the head teacher and others to provide furniture suited to the individual's need. Arithmetic, for example, was taught on a peg board cut out with a bit and fretsaw. Although the present day computer keyboard is infinitely superior, the pupil could learn a feel for wood at the same time. Personally, I have benefited from the attention of specialists and surgeons, but one of my biggest leaps forward was when a craftsman devised a splint for my right arm.

We have already identified one of the trends which has influenced the great development of adaptations. Wood and similar materials are almost obsolete; the technician has taken over from the craftsman and has found that modern materials can do infinitely more than was possible in the past. Many people believe that modern technology has liberated disabled people, and how true this is. But, it tends to be a belief based on a mystique surrounding modernity rather than informed knowledge. Let us, for instance, consider communication. The difficulties of speech impairment and of writing have been largely overcome. Some speech therapists even undergo courses in computing. Computer programs have been developed which allow the severely palsied or paralysed child to communicate using a word processor that responds to eye movements or any other convenient ability. New languages, such as BLISS (which is a mixture of words and symbols, named after its Canadian inventor) now enable spastics who have little or no ability to speak to communicate with an untrained adult. Anyone can understand a BLISS board, and programmed word processors can print normally the codified language of a child using such a code as BLISS.

Electronics have brought other benefits particularly in the area of miniaturisation. A Possum Unit of 10–15 years ago which could undertake several tasks within a house instructed by a series of blowing or sucking, is now replaced by a home computer which is unobtrusive and which can control as many functions as the electrician is capable of switching. Adaptations to cars can now be much more complex because the controls have been reduced in size and made more efficient. In effect, with appropriate willpower and sufficient resources, almost any function can now be programmed for a disabled person except, of course, nursing facilities.

A problem which is very often highlighted by the media is that of resources. Modern technology is expensive and the costs have to be met by someone. Many disabled people can claim that they are caught in a poverty trap, yet many on the other hand have never received so much benefit. These benefits derive from various sources. *First*, for some there are increased state benefits. The British Government has withdrawn benefits in kind, such as invalid cars, and instead has provided a mobility allowance and underwritten finance houses which allow manufacturers to compete in a very lucrative market with all kinds of adaptations to assist mobility in the house and on the road. A *second* source of finance comes from the involvement of statutory bodies and charities who are increasingly concerned with 'community care' as opposed to institutional care. This has resulted in a lucrative market for aids to help with everything from cooking to recreation, from hygiene to hoists which alleviate the back-breaking work formerly the lot of the carers. All these developments are very positive and to be commended, but the market has been almost saturated and the duplication of products and the resultant advertising can lead to unnecessarily high costs and great business turnover. The choice is almost embarrassing, and exhibitions such as NAIDEX (The National Aids Exhibition) and other regional events underscore the degree of competition to sell one's product. At some stage the market will become saturated; some bankruptcies have already occurred or have been averted by takeovers. If money is forthcoming from charities or can be kept within the individual budget of the disabled person, there is no problem; but in my experience there is a financial drain upon the entire family of a disabled person, as those who care most go out of their way to help purchase a car, adapt a house or buy a computer. *Third*, what is the purchaser actually being offered? In the realm of architecture, most adaptations are now subject to Codes of Practice and British Standards,[6] but I would like to see the application of these standards to all products, and in particular to the adaptation of cars.

Finally, we return to resources. There is an unfair distribution of government allowances which the last chapter suggested should be rectified. At present, many go without and the media report upon failures as well as success stories. We applaud and admire the boy who painstakingly writes poetry using a primitive pointing board and typewriter, whilst we know that there are others equally disabled who are writing much faster and more efficiently with the benefit of an electronic communication system of some sort.

Undoubtedly there are a great many riches available to the disabled to enhance their life and their talents, and it is part of our duty as Christians to ensure that these are distributed with fairness and a sense of moral obligation to as many as possible. We must not let our baser instincts run for excessive profit, nor must we allow too much inequality to occur which enhances the talents of some disabled people whilst suppressing those of others who cannot meet the cost.

This chapter has shown to us that the quality of life which we offer to disabled people is dependent upon our attitudes. By our prejudice we can suppress the disabled, by our lack of openness we can close doors, which seldom open twice, in realms which, unless we change, will only be rectified by legislation. And we can affect their quality of life by the way we as individuals, as supporters of charities, and as taxpayers and ratepayers, can choose to supply or deny the modern technological resources which can transform life for so many. If as Christians we live by the dead letter of the law, we can exercise minimal and begrudging care. But if we live by the lively love of Christ, we will foster a spirit of openness and means of enrichment which will further the integration and enlivenment of disabled people.

Notes to Chapter 6

1   E Goffman, *Stigma: Notes on the Management of a Spoiled Identity* (Prentice Hall Inc, New Jersey, 1963)
2   *Report by the Committee on Restrictions Against Disabled People* (CORAD) (DHSS, Crown Copyright, 1982)
3   CORAD, *ibid*
4   CORAD, *ibid*
5   CORAD, *ibid*
6   *DIG's National Disability Income* (Policy Statement, 1987)

7

Disabled People
in the Heart of the Church

In September 1967 I returned from a twenty-first birthday trip to America half-way through my honours course in sociology. I remember sitting at the end of my parent's bed late one night, which is always the time for serious conversations, and announcing that I wanted to study for the ministry. With two years left to go, my mother now saw another three or four years of dictation and writing looming ahead. In common with many friends who were to learn over the next few weeks, they did not know whether to laugh or cry. One very valid doubt was in everyone's mind—could I do it? It was pointed out that it was the most difficult profession a disabled person could undertake, which is a statement so interwoven with myth and practical truth that it is really the topic of this chapter.

However, let us return to America: my involvement with civil rights and my exposure to the Vietnam War seemed to crystallise thoughts which had been flirting with the ministry for years. Even at Communion in Iona Abbey a fortnight after my return, my prayer was, 'God help me to make sense out of this nonsense'. If I were to continue to write in this vein I would be in danger of belittling my Call, but it is vitally important to put it into perspective because people have a tendency to see the disabled believer, especially if he is a minister, through rose-tinted spectacles. Disabled people have found that their disability has inspired a ministry within them, but I do not feel the compulsion of Joni or other similar evangelists. My disability has influenced my Call only in so far as it has shaped my personality.

It is equally important to put into perspective the congregations with whom I have worked. Here again it is a matter of

111

being jocular or taking life too seriously. I remember remarking to my father that all I would ever ask of a congregation would be that they would instal a shower in the manse. My first manse had one and my second congregation installed one! I also suggested that any congregation which called me would indeed be remarkable and special. Experience has taught me that no congregation is thus endowed, but within them there are men and women with imagination and insight. It is to them and to 30 or so Vacancy Committees that this chapter is dedicated.

When a Vacancy Committee, usually a group of 12 ordinary men and women who are elected by a congregation to seek for a minister, gather to meet me, they are faced by a cerebral palsied minister who might as well be wearing a placard saying, 'I am nervous'. They become aware that my speech is far from perfect, my gait is dreadful, that I have no use of my right hand and only partial use of my left. Some were considerate enough to meet over a cup of coffee and soon noticed that I could not lift the cup and had to bend over awkwardly to use a straw. Embarrassment was increased if they asked me to write out a note of my expenses and found that such a task was too laborious to be done immediately. Lest the reader is now tempted to join my mother's friends in tears, let us remember that on at least two occasions these strangers who have encountered my disability have seen beyond it and assisted my call to a charge. From my safe watery haven in Orkney, I can put such mutual ordeals aside for a time. However, it seems important to look at the problems of the disabled person in the ministry through the eyes of the typical Vacancy Committee.

The first problem I imagine disabled ministers encounter is that of pity tinged with a feeling of admiration and uplift on the part of the spectator. It is inadvisable and potentially compromising to offer a disabled person any position or status simply because of their disability. This is particularly so in the case of a minister or anyone with an equally public position. I have heard it said that we may inspire others who are disabled. This, unfortunately, in my experience is not true. I know that many are encouraged by my progress and derive great satisfaction from any association with me, but I am equally aware that the disabled person who has been secularised is unlikely to find faith solely because of my own; people make a mistake in believing that the contrary is true.

There is another area where pity and compassion can distort judgments. Looking at someone's disability can lead a person to misjudge the character of that person. I have found in my own case that the nature of my faith is assumed rather than discerned; it is assumed that I have an evangelistic zeal which has overcome the tremendous odds against which I have supposedly fought, and I constantly have to refer people back to America and my trivial remark on Iona. It annoys me at times that my faith is never called into question and that I seem to slot into any faction within the Church. A minister cannot live on such a high pedestal, and a tumble when it comes is much harder.

Tied in with the whole attitude of pity is a perception of weakness. My congregations have been remarkable in that something in their past has been highly controversial. In the case of Wallace Green, they suffered years of unrest while they debated whether to secede from the Union of the Presbyterian Church of England and the Congregational Union of England and Wales. In the case of Orkney, I doubt if anyone would deny that some bitterness had been engendered by the decision to close one of the churches against the wishes of many of the islanders and by the subsequent decision to restore it almost three years later under the name of St Columba's. I suspect that such controversies breed within a congregation a certain pathology which favours the call of a controversial minister who is perceived either as being indebted to the 'enlightened few' or is likely to allow the situation to continue without interfering because of weakness. This is a firmly held 'gut' feeling which I believe stems from the conclusions which the ordinary person comes to when he encounters disability for the first time without training or background.

This chapter is in a sense a personal manifesto for the future employment of disabled ministers and begins with the plea that no one should confuse issues because they are facing a new situation for the first time. It has already been stated that it is not courage or faith which is the basic quality of a disabled person, but resilience. Weakness is likely to be one of the last of his characteristics. And so I have gone to each church and found that I have upset certain people's preconceptions but fortunately enlightened many more. Having discussed 'pathology', which is unseen and hypothetical, we must turn to the real and sometimes mundane issues of church life.

The presuppositions discussed above can be proved in reality. Since I became a minister I have visited hospitals assiduously and in fact was a hospital chaplain in Berwick. Visiting geriatric wards has frankly always been a nightmare because the generation represented there will be among the last to accept the disabled; and in some cases with second childhood the elderly lose the inhibitions which instil politeness in others. I know from long and difficult experience the comments patients make in 'stage whispers' even before I am out of earshot. 'Isn't it a pity?' 'A man like that shouldn't be doing this kind of work.' 'What an inspiration and how brave he is.' Unwittingly these old people betray the confusions which others are bound to feel but suppress. In their own way they do not wish to deal with further confusions on top of those imposed by the hospital regime. Just as children can be won over very successfully, so can old folk. By perseverance I know that I can now spend a very loving hour in a geriatric ward.

I have also discovered that if you explain disability to children they respond warmly and positively. The children of Hoy know that different parts of the brain 'post letters' to all parts of the body, but that in my case my 'sorting office' is not very well managed and the 'letters' end up going to the wrong address. They are encouraged to believe that as the brain learns more and more 'post codes', less 'mail' goes astray. That is the type of impressionable story which may last a lifetime and radically alter the conversation in some geriatric ward of the future.

Understandably, Vacancy Committees and others question most closely the visible signs of capability to undertake a task. Can he climb our stairs? How will someone so disabled cope with wind and snow and ice, not to mention boats? How will this man manage to write, they ask, when they have just seen and commented upon the answer? It is obvious to most that I have no notes in the pulpit and very few at meetings unless it is a matter of record. This book is not my choice of medium; I am a man of the spoken word not the written word, and I am often embarrassed by that fact because having had to dictate all my life I tend to take spelling for granted. I can actually spell in French better than in English because the examination board insisted that I spell French words when dictating but took my English for granted.

When it comes to these general matters all people who are looking at a disabled person must try to acknowledge that he has a certain amount of integrity. In other words if he says he can do a job, he can do it. Other qualities might mitigate against him when compared to other applicants, but to question the rudiments is to make an unintentional slur on his personality. No one in Orkney now questions my ability to get on and off boats provided I am satisfied with the safety. It is for that reason that I had to agree maturely that a small island called Graemsay was unsuitable to be part of my charge and the Presbytery calmly and decisively transferred it to another suitable charge. Another resolve I would plead for, therefore, is that churchmen and women realise that it is possible to make realistic assessment of a disabled person's capabilities, provided they can discuss with him how certain problems can be shared in the ministry of Word and Sacraments.

The ministry of Word and Sacrament is essentially different from any other occupation. It is based entirely on performance and cannot be influenced or changed by technology. When a disabled person applies for a sedentary office job the main questions to be asked concern the access of the office, the type of telephone to be installed and the space within which a wheelchair can be manoeuvred. Adaptations can be readily provided by employers, either through the Manpower Services Commission or any other means. However, no such adaptations are available outside the disabled minister's study. Once he has entered the church of his choosing, which presumably is suited to his capabilities, it is the performance of ministry which must be adapted. This is where the Vacancy Committees and the generally curious do not know where to start questioning, or perhaps feel that questions would be inappropriate.

I believe that it is important that congregations consider carefully how weddings and funerals are going to be conducted and, most importantly, the Sacraments. It is relatively simple to understand how a static and well loved congregation can come to know and understand their disabled minister. Such a loving and obliging relationship cannot however be taken for granted, because the Church of Scotland, in common with many other Churches, has far too many occasional services which prevents it from becoming a purely congregational Church. Guests arriving at a wedding, or mourners at a funeral, are possibly meeting myself or any other disabled minister for the first time; they have not called him nor are they emotionally equipped to deal with both the *rite de passage* and the encounter with disability at the same time.

In both instances there are certain techniques which can be adopted. I have always made a point of entering the church as it fills for both weddings and funerals. I make myself obvious by opening the Bible, laying out my books, checking positioning of participants and so forth, in order that I may be seen. My entry into the church to conduct the service is therefore not my first appearance.[1] Such a technique has been portrayed by Goffman in his book *Stigma*. My own technique is based on common sense. In order that the congregation may become attuned to my voice, I always have a very short Call to Worship followed immediately by a hymn. If I am aware that I am going to have to make a move in the course of the service, I move during a hymn when congregations are likely to be looking at the text of their hymnary.

All these techniques are supplemented by certain basic emotional instincts within people. I am convinced that whilst mourners wish their dear ones to be committed with the greatest of dignity they also appreciate seeing that the officiating minister can also be disturbed and can mourn as they do. Hard as I may try I cannot always conceal my emotions or stress. I have noticed also that the most successful weddings are ones where the family know me well and they have shared the difficulties beforehand. The bride and groom are usually so relaxed that they can easily smile through their excitement. Cerebral palsy is characterised by three basic symptoms of which two are important in this context. I suffer from athetosis and whenever I find myself in a stressful situation, involuntary movements increase. Other cerebral palsied people are spastic and become more stiff, less fluent when under stress. In each case the only cure is practice, and I believe that I have practised now for 14 years and have overcome many of the difficulties which I have to face.

Moving more rapidly to the ministry of the Word, it has been pointed out to me that my spastic voice has certain dramatic features and lends itself well to public speaking. On a good day many flaws in my speech can be concealed or turned to dramatic advantage in the course of preaching. The most annoying thing about any ordinary or special service is that I cannot have an 'off-day'. An 'off-day' is perceived as being the fault of my disability, when I am aware that it can be caused by anything from a row at home to a lack of conviction in one's subject matter.

Jesus gave us the Sacraments as visible signs of his gospel of grace. They are not spoken but are performed, and they do not belong to the realm of the cerebral but to the response of the emotions. The Word which has been understood and inwardly digested is now set so that we may enjoy the gift of God, in the seal of his love in Baptism, or in the offer of the means of grace in the Lord's Supper. Both these Sacraments have to be performed by myself and have required more courage and understanding than anything on the part of elders and myself. Yet never have these been openly discussed by a Vacancy Committee, nor indeed by many churchmen.

I deal with Baptism very simply. I first of all reassure the parents that I am not going to drop their child on its head, and I ask the father to hold the child whilst I sprinkle water in the name of the Father, and of the Son, and of the Holy Spirit. As I have come to recognise my own child's movements, so now I can interplay with the baby much more successfully, holding his hand for the blessing or risking gestures or smiles. The actions of a disabled minister become very deliberate and accentuated and actually increase the solemnity of that moment in the celebration of the Sacrament. So often I have envied in the past ministers who are 'good' with babies, but now I realise the value of concentrating the mind of the congregation on the symbolic washing with water.

'In the Eucharist we Christians concentrate our motive and act out the theory of human living'.[2] The motive of a civilisation is that which marks it as brutal or kind, respective or free thinking. The theory of human living behind it is our willingness to open our churches and our hearts to all the victims of our civilisation. Within the Eucharist or the Lord's Supper lies the mystery of God's love, his desire that we should come together as one partaking of the same spiritual food, and learning of the same grace within the Gospel of Jesus Christ our Lord. For many centuries men have been privileged to preside at the table of the Lord and invite men and women from east and west to come and feast at the table which is set before them. The gravity of this act, this liturgy, is immense and is part of the building up of the fellowship which takes place in the daily celebration, or in great feasts of thanksgiving four times a year or even less frequently. It has the power to hold men and women close to their Lord and to fellow human beings in the privacy of solitary confinement, or to bring together hundreds of strangers under one roof seeking to serve one King and to rejoice at his presence. This simple act is the central tradition which has been handed down to us, not to be spoken but enacted principally by two simple movements of the human hand in the breaking of bread and in the pouring and serving of wine. I continually have to ask myself: How is this act possible for one who cannot break bread, nor raise the chalice?

For generations Christians have looked for comfort and security in this celebration. They have been aware that changes in words and in actions will only occur after careful deliberation and reflection. A disabled minister coming to this celebration may not have had time to reflect on the changes which he is about to institute to accommodate the particular circumstances of a congregation and their environment.

The first thing that has to be said is that this act, this Sacrament, can be very significant or quite insignificant. Not all Church of Scotland ministers are sacramentalist, and other denominations of the reformed tradition can place even less stress on these celebrations. John Knox and the founding fathers of the Church of Scotland had little intention of denying the centrality of the Sacraments, but time and tradition have succeeded in doing this. It is therefore of little surprise that so few Vacancy Committees, so few elders within the Church, are actually concerned with the problems posed in my own situation. Lax practice and little understanding is no excuse for shirking the most important question to face a disabled minister: How can he share in the Sacramental life of the Church?

The Sacrament which came to us as a tradition from our Lord himself is a personal tradition. Jesus with all his competence turned the Jewish feast into a memorial in which he set forth himself. It was done without aid or assistance, and the effort which must have gone into this Last Supper was to be over-shadowed by the individual effort of facing up to and dying on the cross. Can I as a disabled minister succeed in a personal celebration of the Lord's Supper? The answer is inevitably no, I must share it with those with whom I have been given a trust and a relationship. When it comes to breaking the bread it is an elder standing by my left hand who will break it and hold it up for the congregation to see, and an elder on my right hand who will lift the cup as I point to it and pronounce the words, 'This is the blood of Christ shed for many, drink ye all of it'. These elders then serve me with both the bread and wine. Such a practice I believe to be acceptable to my congregations.

I have a constant fear of being asked to celebrate the Sacrament of the Lord's Supper outwith my own congregation. Travelling to another church within the Presbytery, or to the Guild, means that I leave my well trusted elders behind and the safe acceptance of my congregation. Suffice to say that within the Church of Scotland I have never yet been discouraged or dismayed by the response of strangers. I have indeed had to celebrate the Sacrament at almost a moment's notice through a mix up within my diary, and the Guildswomen of Duns Presbyterial Council showed remarkable adaptability. Yet it remains a fear because I believe that there are many churches where I could not successfully conduct the Sacrament without causing some offence.

I have already hinted that I believe that the Church of Scotland is an accommodating Church. I would question whether disabled ministers and priests would meet the same understanding within the Anglican Communion or the Roman Catholic Church. I have attended a Eucharist within a Priory of Dominican Monks and found that it was celebrated by an old man with deeply shrivelled hands who suffered greatly from arthritis. As in my own case, so with this brother; he was acting in a position of trust and mutual acceptance. It would indeed be gratifying to know to what extent others have been accepted; and to know this not from a denomination which can claim to be Sacramental or non-Sacramental in outlook, but from the deepest Sacramentalist.

I believe that the position of the disabled demands that a liturgy should be developed, not for them, but in order that they may be included. The Roman Catholic Church has managed to include mentally handicapped people as Servers in the simple repetitive ritualistic acts without which the Sacrament would be incomplete. I believe that other denominations can also accommodate the disabled minister or elder by offering to them the opportunity to transcend their physical disability by bringing the entire fellowship closer together in a way which minimises the apparent difficulty with movement. It is so easy to concentrate upon the difficulties that it becomes impossible for the disabled minister to embark upon a celebration with the purity of heart and the solemnity which the Sacrament demands.

I believe that we must develop a new liturgy in which disabled people can join in or lead. We must devise a liturgy of concelebration which allows a handicapped person to act equally and in unison with someone who has an equal status and rôle within this celebration. The nearest I have ever come to it was at a Student Christian Movement gathering at Swanwick, in Derbyshire. At that celebration we all stood in a circle, each one of us spoke the words, and one member picked up the bread, and another the wine, and we could all rejoice in our celebration. The radicalism of the SCM in the sixties may not be the answer for today, but I believe that this gathering together around the table which has been so central to our tradition may be rediscovered to the benefit of all, not least the disabled members of a congregation.

The practice was readopted by George MacLeod many years ago in the Good Friday celebration in Iona Abbey, and a recent article in a journal on church architecture extolled the virtue of the long Communion tables and pews exemplified in Ardchatten Church and other parts of the West Highlands and in at least one church which I know in Orkney.[3] Those mentioned were not suitable for disabled people, but the free and movable seating of churches such as Rutherford in Aberdeen leaves ample opportunity to accommodate the disabled around the table whether as members or presiding as elders or ministers. It is interesting that the article on the long table was aimed at an English readership and that the Church of England has unwittingly taken steps in the right direction by recognising the value of Henry Moore's sculptured Communion table in St Stephen's Church, Walbrook, London. The essence of all these architectural features is that it draws members of a congregation together in a way which has been lost in the pews and which, because we are not facing one another, allows us to forget the disadvantaged in our fellowship.

If the Church decides that modifications are desirable both in architecture and in liturgical practice, it must *ipso facto* accept that the disabled constitute a special case. Disabled people should, and could be, given a rôle within the service of the Church—in the ministry of Jesus Christ. They are endowed with insights which ought to be heard and understood, and many have found that this is in fact their ministry. The guiding insight which appears to emerge is a desire to inspire. Most literature connected with disability in the Church is of an inspirational nature and there seems to be a compulsion on the part of all Christians to publicise the best which is brought out by or in a disabled person. However, I have been at pains to point out that inspiration can lead to many misunderstandings, and a mistaken perception of the disabled. A burden can be imposed upon them by those who look to them for inspiration. It is seen in the way that many cannot cope with so called heroism or can become paranoid or have inflated egos when they are constantly showered with congratulatory praise. People's continuous remarks about the courage or determination of a disabled individual can lead to all sorts of personality problems.

There are three problems which may face the disabled Christian. *First,* Christian ministers should bear the message of the Gospel as their conscience dictates. This means that there is a great variety in the way the message is put forward and this often results in divisions and much debate. So be it. The *second* means of communication is to be found in the way any Christian conducts his life; many a quiet and modest deed speaks volumes about the Gospel. However, disabled people carry the message in a *third* way; their success in attaining an office within the Church unwittingly becomes a source of inspiration. The problem is that the disabled person has no control over this message with the result that what is preached may not be in harmony with the perceived message emanating from disability. Thus, certain groups or congregations may adopt a disabled person by assuming that their understanding of him is actually the same as the message which he may wish to put across himself. The two may be vastly different. We must seek to understand disabled people plainly for what they have to say and how their beliefs are carried into everyday life.

It would be possible to conclude that our chief obligation is to let disabled people be as they are, yet I believe that they have a rôle to play which must not be lost.

A completely different rôle must be devised, drawing on the potential which has been pointed out in this book but has not been consciously utilised by society at large or the Church in particular. The rôle of disabled people in the service of the Church most fruitfully develops into that of 'liberating educator'. Both these words have to be explained and I believe that they point the way to a ministry suitable for disabled people, based on a realistic assessment of their own potentialities and personalities. By 'liberating' I mean that we must present, as Christ did, ways in which conventions of the day may be fruitfully broken, so that something new may be developed. By 'educator' I mean that others must perceive the advantage of this and act accordingly.

The process can be seen (a) biblically, (b) theologically and (c) socially. (a) Biblically we have the gradual acceptance of disabled people into the midst of the Christian fellowship. From the rigid position of Leviticus we move to the liberated acceptance of Jesus Christ; and throughout Christian history we see the weight of burdens being lifted both from the disabled and those who looked on with guilt, who wished to shut away the blind child or would not have carried the paralytic into the crowded house. God's glory has been revealed in his acceptance of disabled people. (b) Theologically, we are already witnessing Christian scholars grappling with conventions which are barriers to the advancement of women, and, where conventions do not matter, the Church is responding to the needs of women. Eventually all denominations will ordain them. But the theological stripping of convention is a slow and painful process and requires greater faith than most of us have. In most instances of social education our intellects acknowledge the new state of affairs more readily than emotions and traditions. This is true of various discriminations which the Church exhibits. And (c), socially, in all of this it is the weakness of those disabled who are already in the Church which will count; it is their determination to break barriers and to force change which will help others in the future. It is significant alas that many, including myself, are not militant and are disinclined to alter convention in such a way that would lead to discomfiture.

The Church is actually very conscious of categories. Within the councils of the world Church and the national Church we find that members are divided by sex, age, lay or ordained, and by many other criteria. I feel that having worked with such categories on several committees within the Church of Scotland, it is now time to consider disabled people as a special category and to realise their unique contribution.

This contribution will only be brought out of people who have the potential but need encouragement by a special ministry. However, their reluctance to become militant is reinforced by an innate desire to conform and often to overcompensate in doing so. It is incumbent on those who have vision to see the new potential and to articulate it. It is for this reason that I advocate a ministry to and for disabled people. I believe that the world of disability is so different from the normal world that the need to categorise it is the only way in which advanced understanding can be attained.

There are two ways in the Church of Scotland through which a ministry or an experiment can be formulated. The *first* way is to pioneer the experiment and, after proving its value, appeal to the Assembly to support it through one or other of its committees. The *second* way is to mount a full frontal assault on the General Assembly and convince it of the need for whatever move one has in mind. Both ways are being made more difficult by budgeting restraints and by procedural restraints designed to protect the budgets of committees. I believe that both these routes are not at present fully open to disabled people. As already stated, the General Assembly is a forbidding gathering for one who is disabled. The words of Kristine Gibbs express exactly how I felt at one General Assembly in particular:

> 'I put the paper on the lectern. My vision swam and my knees were knocking so hard that I was sure that people could see. "Act it, act it." Straightening myself to my full height, very slowly and clearly I began: "Madam Chairman and colleagues, I will speak very briefly and I hope to the point". The room was completely silent, hushed as people began to realise the limitations imposed by my disability.'[4]

Both physically and emotionally the General Assembly of the Church of Scotland is exhausting. There is no accommodation for anyone with a disability affecting their mobility, little regard for wheelchairs and no regard at all for easy access to the podium. These visible signs of rejection should be the first priority of the Church for improvement and this could then lead to the possibility of a real debate. I spoke at the Assembly on the need to think of disability in the International Year of the Disabled Person, but felt that I had entered the debating chamber by the 'back door'. In other words, it was more by accident than by design that I was in fact able to take a place in the body of the General Assembly and to struggle to the lectern, as one daily newspaper put it when I spoke on another occasion. Disabled people must be brought in by the 'front door', invited in by the openness of the environment and by the eagerness of the Assembly to hear what they have to say. The other way is to invite disabled people to sit on committees; this would require that the

Church Offices were made accessible to disabled people and that the Nomination Committee felt compelled to discriminate positively in their favour.

Assuming that one of these routes was made available to myself or another disabled person, what would we stress as a suitable ministry to and for disabled people?

A New Ministry

The most important feature of any argument would be to stress the positive. Many ministers, members and congregations are deeply involved with the disabled. I remember being pushed to church in a wheelchair from Westerlea, and I know that such involvement in Murrayfield, Edinburgh with the activities of Westerlea and the Scottish Council for Spastics continues to this day. I am aware that I presented a problem to the ladies who took me to church and often taxed their sensitivity in my questioning, and the physical disturbance which this caused me. I found participating in a service so strenuous that, even into my thirties, it was like joining in a wrestling match for the one who was trying to control my movements. I am convinced that throughout Scotland other people have seen similar manifestations of the emotional stress worship can place upon the disabled person. Week by week members of congregations are encountering disabled people who live in homes or sheltered housing, and ministers are faithfully visiting such places as chaplains or friends. However, I believe that men and women with particular gifts in identifying the stressful nature of disability could act as support in sharing their psychological knowledge of emotion. A theology of disability does not stem from skill or knowledge but from the painful conquering of disabling manifestations within the Church. A peripatetic minister could help all these establishments and also bring Christ into sheltered workshops and training centres. As a Church we expect to have chaplains in industry, why not in this sphere as well?

My next argument is that the Church must be actively seen to be concerned with the welfare of disabled people. The Church's voice has to be heard in councils for the disabled, in welfare organisations and at a government level. I would suggest that the first committee of the Church of Scotland to be asked to have a disabled member by right should be Church and Nation.

Next I would argue that we require more church services which focus on disability. It is a boost to morale for the disabled and their loved ones to meet together in an atmosphere of worship. In 15 years I have only taken part in three such services. The church would probably become confused about the specific purpose of such services. I believe that many would wish to engage in a ministry of healing. This is a very proper type of service, but I have advocated a theology of disability which stresses wholeness and acceptance. Such a message in a service does not result in healing but offers a faith and an acceptance born of an understanding of the love of God demonstrated to all through the suffering and love of God's Son.

Finally, it would be a great source of comfort to many ministers to know that there was someone they could consult themselves or refer disabled people to in order that problems which they felt were too difficult to solve personally, could be handed over to a specialist.

Churches in Britain cannot afford to lag behind the Americans and many other countries in realising that 'inclusiveness' is not a quality of Church life only to be attained by women, but by the whole spectrum of society, not least by disabled people and their families.

Notes to Chapter 7

1   E Goffman, *Stigma: Notes on the Management of a Spoiled Identity*
2   Dom Gregory Dix, *The Shape of the Liturgy* (A & C Black, London, 1945), p 752
3   David H Maxwell, 'Church of Scotland—The Architectural Heritage' from *Church Building* (Summer, 1986)
4   Kristine Gibbs, *Only One Way Up*, p 144

Epilogue

In the late sixties I used to join a small group for supper and for Communion in the Chaplain's flat in the University of Edinburgh. The Georgian terraced houses of George Square retain a secret which I wish to share as part of my journey towards acceptance. I went with a dread of these Communions because I knew how physically distraught I was going to be and how dependent I would be on one or two girls (it has always got to be the opposite sex!). I consider it a tribute to his faith that the Chaplain, Andrew Morton, saw through and beyond this struggle and was prepared to write a reference when I applied for the ministry. I have to this day an unfulfilled ambition to preside at a Communion with some of that group, thus rewarding faith and rejoicing in acceptance. That ambition may never come true but still I can rejoice in the rewards of Orkney.

Later this year I have been commissioned to sail into the Pentland Firth in the Longhope lifeboat to commit ashes to the deep. Sometime in the course of the year I will no doubt fly in an eight seater aircraft to at least one of the northern isles, and I will certainly fly to Edinburgh several times. On these occasions I will reflect on how fortunate I am to be able to combine enjoyment of the sea and the elements with my vocation. I realise how lucky I am to be part of the Church of Scotland and to have been accepted as a minister.

Looking at my own situation and at no other, I see little cause for militancy, for vast schemes of reform; but I do believe that if we are going to be responsible to disabled people and meet their needs fairly and squarely, we must indeed attempt to reform ourselves. One brief look at the introduction of this book will show the reader how fortunate I am. I know many disabled people who have been equally fortunate and many who have been less so. I am touched by some of their gentle ways of accepting their disability, but I am also challenged by those who are really quite militant in their call for a more just society. It is when I remind myself of these calls that I become aware that existing Christian literature upon disability will not satisfy, that we must face the issue reasonably and look to other countries for inspiration. There is little or no compensation in being disabled except for enlisting the help and the acceptance of others. Do not be deceived by the good fortune of disabled people who can publicise their situation and their plight, but rather be challenged by the silence of the majority who cannot articulate their frustrations and their discontent.

It would be the mark of a caring Church to solemnly declare that they must embark on a project to welcome disabled people with faith and acceptance into fellowship with Jesus Christ, who has identified with their plight and who will through grace show us all the way forward.

Appendix

This appendix contains names and addresses of useful organisations relating to the disabilities mentioned in this book. Where possible both the Scottish and English based organisations are given.

A comprehensive list can be found in the *Directory for Disabled People* (fourth edition), compiled by Ann Darnbrough and Derek Kinrade. Published in conjunction with The Royal Association for Disability and Rehabilitation.

General Information
Scottish Council on Disability
 5 Shandwick Place, Edinburgh EH2 4RG (tel. 031 229 8632)
Royal Association for Disability and Rehabilitation (RADAR)
 25 Mortimer Street, London W1N 8AB (tel. 01 637 5400)
Disablement Income Group (DIG)
 Scotland ECAS House, 28–30 Howden Street, Edinburgh
 EH8 9HW (tel. 031 667 0249 or 668 3577)
Disablement Income Group Charitable Trust
 Millmead Business Centre, Millmead Road, London
 N17 9QU (tel. 01 801 8013)

Charities related to certain disabilities
Arthritis and Rheumatism Council
 41 Eagle Street, London WC1 4AR (tel. 01 405 8572)

Association for Spina Bifida and Hydrocephalus (ASBAH)
 22 Upper Woburn Place, London WC1H OEP (tel. 01 388
 1382)
Scottish Spina Bifida Association
 190 Queensferry Road, Edinburgh EH4 2BW (tel. 031 332
 0743)

Cystic Fibrosis Research Trust
  5 Blyth Road, Bromley, Kent BR1 3RS (tel. 01 464 7211)
  Scottish Council Offices, 39 Hope Street, Glasgow G2 6AE
  (tel. 041 226 4244)

Down's Children's Association
  12–13 Clapham Common Southside, London SW4 7AA
  (tel. 01 720 0008)
Scottish Down's Syndrome Association
  54 Shandwick Place, Edinburgh EH2 4RT (tel. 031 226
  2420)

Multiple Sclerosis Society of Great Britain and Northern
    Ireland
  286 Munster Road, London SW6 6AP (tel. 01 381 4022/
  4025 or 01 385 6146/7/8)
Association of Scottish Branches
  27 Castle Street, Edinburgh EH2 3DN (tel. 031 225 3600)
Northern Ireland Branch
  34 Annadale Avenue, Belfast BT7 3JJ (tel. 0232 648379)

Muscular Dystrophy Group of Great Britain and Northern
    Ireland
  Nattrass House, 35 Macaulay Road, London SW4 OQP
  (tel. 01 720 8055)

Scottish Council for Spastics
  'Rhumore', 22 Corstorphine Road, Edinburgh EH12 6HP
  (tel. 031 337 9876)
The Spastics Society
  12 Park Crescent, London W1N 4EQ (tel. 01 636 5020)

Index

131